———— The Ministry of Sanctification: Book I ————
LOOSE THEM AND LET THEM GO

Earn J. Flowers
Rt. 1 Box 243J
1-904-643-5232
Bristol, Fla. 32321

The Ministry of Sanctification: Book I
LOOSE THEM AND LET THEM GO
by
Earn J. and Gloria Flowers

The Flowers Ministry
Bristol, Florida

FATHER & SON
PUBLISHING

Unless otherwise indicated, all Scripture quotations are taken from the *King James Version* of the Bible. Some quotations are from *The Holy Bible, New International Version* (NIV). Copyright © 1973, 1978 by the International Bible Society. Used by permission of Zondervan Bible Publishers. Other quotations are from *The Amplified Bible* (AMP) containing the *Amplified Old Testament* and the *Amplified New Testament*. Copyright © 1965 by Zondervan Publishing House, Grand Rapids, Michigan.

Loose Them and Let Them Go
ISBN 0-942407-11-3
Copyright © 1987 by
Earn J. Flowers
Route 1, Box 243F
Bristol, Florida 32321
Artwork by William Brannon, Niceville, FL
Cover design by Deborah Reeves, Bristol, FL

Printed in the United States of America.
All rights reserved under International Copyright Law.
Contents and-or cover may not be reproduced in whole or in part in any form without the express written consent of the author.

CONTENTS

Dedication   vii
Foreword: Dr. Bill Hamon   ix
Preface: The Purpose of Sanctification   xiii
Introduction: Personal Experiences   xix

Part I: Sanctification and Deliverance   1
  1. Why Do Christians Need Sanctification?   5
  2. "Holes" and "Cracks" in the Wineskin of the Soul   15
  3. Can a Christian Have an Evil Spirit?   23
  4. The Curse Causeless Shall Not Come   29
  5. How Do We Give Place to the Devil?   39
  6. Detestable Things   45
  7. How to Tell the True From the False   57
  8. The Unholy Trinity   67
  9. The Authority of the Believer   83

Part II: Workbook for Sanctification/Deliverance   93
  10. The Path to Freedom   95
  11. The Prayer of Sanctification: Sequence
      and Procedure   103
  12. Standing in the Gap   111

Appendix: Sanctification Worksheets   117
Bibliography   129
About the Author   133

Dedication

This book is dedicated to the memory of the late Burnie Davis of Burnie Davis Global Ministries, Pueblo, Colorado, a well-known missionary evangelist to India, Mexico, and countries in Central and South America for many years. He also authored a book on the operation of miracles in ministry.[1] In 1973, he taught me how to believe and act on the Word of God.

At one of his meetings, I asked him, "How can I get involved in working in the ministry and praying for people and seeing miracles happen like you do?"

He said, "The reason I am doing it and you are not is because I am doing it and you are not!"

Then he prayed a simple prayer for me, and it seemed as if the Word of God came alive to me for the first time. Later, I became an intercessor for his ministry. In 1982, I spent time with him in Belize, Central America. His ministry had the most impact on my life of any of the great ministries that I have known, been involved with, or read after—with one exception: Dr. L. M. Thorne.

Therefore, this book is also dedicated to Dr. Thorne of Abundant Life Church, Fort Walton Beach, Florida, under whom I received my early training in the ministry. I cannot express enough appreciation for these two men who encouraged me the most in my ministry.

Jimmy Flowers
Bristol, Florida
September 5, 1988

Foreword

God is very resourceful. For every problem, He has an answer; for every need, He has a provision.

For William Booth, He had a dream . . . multitudes drowning in the sea as others called to them from the refuge of a large rock. Yet call as they might, the people chose instead to perish in the tumultuous waters. Shaken from this revelation, Mr. Booth felt compelled to reach out to lost souls who were floudering in sin without accepting help from those who were heralding the gospel of The Rock, Christ Jesus. As a result, the Salvation Army was founded, and since its founding in the 19th century, has made an orchestrated effort to win souls for Christ.

To Pastor Jimmy Flowers, God has given wisdom and understanding. *Loose Them and Let Them Go* affirms the necessity of this first step into the Kingdom of God where we are cleansed from sin.

But this book takes us further into the gospel message and shows us there is help for Christians who are floundering in the sea of sinful living with carnality, attitudes, and sins that prevent them from serving God fully. In this book, we learn how to go beyond this stage into sanctification, and like Lazarus, have our grave clothes removed to walk in newness of life.

The famous reformer Martin Luther, when referring to temptation from the enemy is credited with saying:

"I can't stop the birds from flying over my head, but I can keep them from nesting in my hair."

This book might be best understood as an education in locating the nesting enemy in the lives of others to bring deliverance and cleansing to them.

Every cave explorer knows that even after the bats are gone, there is still a considerable mess left behind. Pastor Flowers offers a balanced treatment in driving off the demonic powers at work in an individual's life *and* cleansing the temple of the filth that remains.

Attempting to administer sanctification without first dealing with root causes would be an exercise in futility. We are not led down a primrose path believing that all our problems can be blamed on the devil and that deliverance is all we need to live upright before God. This volume also effectively identifies and deals with primary root problems such as sin, hurts, wounds, rejection, and rebellion so that sanctification will take place.

The reader will appreciate the quality treatment given the subject of deliverance. We have had much of the extremes: the "demon-behind-every-tree" mentality on the one hand and blatant skepticism concerning demonic spirits on the other.

Loose Them and Let Them Go readily acknowledges the activity and power which demons may exert on the believer, but

Foreword

it does not assume that every ungodliness can be blamed on the devil. We are shown our own responsibility in the matter of sanctification so that the wineskins of our souls are healthy and ably bearing new wine.

Dr. Bill Hamon
President and Founder
Christian International Ministries
and Network of Prophetic Ministries
Point Washington, Florida
September 2, 1988

Preface
The Purpose of Sanctification

In the first half of this century, the phrase, "Saved, sanctified, and filled with the Holy Spirit," was common in Pentecostal and Holiness churches. In the late eighteenth century and the nineteenth centuries, it was an integral part of the Methodist and Methodist-related churches. Now, it is heard in only a few churches. Sanctification has gone out of style. However, the Lord has led me to minister in this area, although in a rather different way than the old-time "tarrying at the altar" or "praying through." Sanctification, as the Lord has led me to minister, starts with confessing anything that is not of God in one's life as *sin*, then asking for and receiving forgiveness.

Many Christians today seem to think that *holiness* is old-fashioned and somehow "legalistic," but that is because the term—in most of our minds—is associated with the "clothesline preaching" that the devil managed to turn *holiness* into. However, that kind of preaching (which was mostly to women) was Pharisaism, the very kind of thing against which

Jesus taught! *Holiness, or sanctification* simply means allowing oneself to be cleansed by the Holy Spirit of the patterns, habits, and thinking of this world's systems.

Other Christians are satisfied with their worldly thinking and believe perfection of the soul will only occur in Heaven or along with the body at the resurrection. The Kenya international director of Full Gospel Business Men's Fellowship International tells of the time when his wife died for a whole day and came back from Heaven with a message from the Lord for him:

> "Son, I am going to send you to many parts of the world. You are to tell everyone without compromise that *sanctification is not done in Heaven, but right here on earth.*"[2]

A few people have objected to this ministry because their understanding of sanctification does not include deliverance. Others have objected on the grounds that associating deliverance with sanctification is "new." But because *you* have never heard of something does not mean it is new. It simply means you have "a lack of knowledge"—which Hosea 4:6 says destroys us.

The best way to handle something "new" in ministry is to do a thorough study of the scriptures being used to see if they are taken out of context or misinterpreted. Seek the Lord for a witness in your spirit as to the truth of this "new word." However, if your mind is so set on other doctrines that you cannot hear clearly and you are uncertain as to the interpretation of the verses involved, simply lay what you have heard aside, and trust the Lord to reveal its truth or error to you in due time.

Our ministry is only new in this particular form. What the Lord has assigned us to do is a combination of deliverance, total repentance of carnality or "soul" power, renewing of the mind, and physical healing—in other words, healing of the spirit, soul, *and* body. Also, it involves the tearing

The Purpose of Sanctification

down of strongholds that give place to the devil. (2 Cor. 10:4, Eph. 4:27.)

Before the Lord led me into this present ministry, I would see some people helped by my preaching or teaching but others would go away hurt and despondent. My heart would break over their conditions, and I began to pray and seek the Lord about how to *really* meet people's needs. God began to show me that most ministries helped set people free from the "snare of the devil," or getting them born again, (2 Tim. 2:26), but did not help them become sanctified. Therefore people still had problems in their souls and bodies. Then He spoke this to me:

"I want you to start ministering sanctification. It will include healing of the broken-hearted, but primarily it will involve cleansing of the body, the soul, and the spirit. There will be inner healing, healing of memories, and healing of the physical body. But for real sanctification to be effective, the people will have to confess things" (attitudes, reactions, and behavior) "as sins and get forgiveness. These things allowed the devil to work in their lives in the first place. If you will do that, I will bless those who do not rebel against Me and who will work with you, and I will cause them in turn to be a blessing to My people wherever they go."

I began to apply the principles in this book as they were revealed to me, and I began to see them work. Then the Lord called Gloria to work with me as a team after our children were grown. Other ministries called "prayer-counseling" combine some of the same areas that our ministry covers but each uses different approaches.

One such ministry was that of the late Agnes Sanford, noted author and teacher.[3] She taught the authority of the believer and that healing and signs and wonders are for today as early as Dr. Kenneth Hagin. However, she is better known in mainline churches. A similar ministry was started by a woman named Anne White.[4] Her prayer-counseling ministry is used in many Assembly of God churches as well as in mainline churches.

Dr. Dennis Bennett and his wife, Rita, have a similar ministry.[5] They appear on Trinity Broadcasting Network (TBN) regularly. He was the first minister to be moved from his church post for being baptized in the Holy Spirit in modern times. The Bennetts say people's minds are so contaminated with the occult—especially through television and the entertainment media—that whenever they lead someone to Christ, they take that person through deliverance *before* getting them baptized in the Holy Spirit. The Bennetts even do this when they give an invitation for salvation to a television audience. Many Christians who need that step of deliverance, however, have never been taken through it. Most of them do not even realize they need it.

Yet another such ministry is John and Paula Sandford's *Elijah House* ministry.[6] All of these ministries pray in tongues and rely on the Holy Spirit to show them specific areas in which a believer needs help. The thing that is different is the method each uses. One ministry may have counselors who ask you the story of your life. As you talk, they note down areas quickened to them by the Holy Spirit. Another ministry simply deals with common problems today—unforgiveness, sexual sins, abortion, the occult, and so forth.

The Lord called us to be "general practitioners," not specialists. The approach Jesus opened to us was to list everything the Lord has revealed through prayer, Bible study, research of others' ministry, and to take every person seeking help through everything in order not to leave any hole for the devil. We believe Jesus called this ministry "sanctification" because it involves *all* of the helps God has provided to bring believers into His righteousness and because it begins with a cleansing of the soul.

Ministries (in addition to those of Dr. L. M. Thorne and the late Burnie Davis) whose revelation knowledge and materials we use include those of the late E. W. Kenyon; and the late

The Purpose of Sanctification

F. F. Bosworth; Frank and Ida Hammond of Plainview, Texas; Win Worley of Highland, Indiana; Don Basham of Illyria, Ohio; Maxwell Whyte of Ontario, Canada; T. L. Osborn of Tulsa, Oklahoma; Charles and Frances Hunter of Kingwood, Texas; and Ernest Gruen of Kansas City, Kansas. (For publications by these ministers and others, see the Bibliography.)

Purpose of Sanctification Ministry

The purpose of our ministry is to help people allow the Holy Spirit to bring about a cleansing of their souls by leading them through several steps:

1. *Renouncing* past involvements in things of Satan, even things that may have seemed harmless at the time. (Deut. 18:10-12.)
2. *Forgiving* anyone against whom they have resentment, bitterness, or hatred — including themselves. (Luke 6:37, 1 John 1:9.)
3. *Breaking* all bondages. (2 Pet. 2:19.)
4. *Casting out* any evil spirits that may have entered through these things. (Mark 16:17.)
5. *Receiving* healing in all the areas of past hurt in order that spirit, soul, and body may be sanctified. (1 Thess. 5:23, 1 Pet. 2:24.)

The purpose is to help Christians get free of any evil spirits and strongholds built by reactions to events in their lives that make legal places for those spirits to dwell. Ephesians was written to Christians, and Paul said, **Neither give place** (a foothold) **to the devil** (Eph. 4:27.) Salvation, healing, and sanctification was provided by Jesus two thousand years ago on the cross. But each person must *receive* salvation in order to obtain a new spirit and be born again as a true child of God. Similarly, each Christian must *receive* healing and sanctification for the soul to be effectively renewed or restored to the image of Christ.

In our sanctification sessions, as well as in the counseling sessions and the healing sessions, *Jesus is magnified*. My wife, Gloria, and I work together as a team, but we never allow the client to focus on us. Jesus is the Healer and the Deliverer, and the Holy Spirit is the Counselor. We are simply the instruments, the vessels, whom God is using. All the glory goes to Jesus.

The ministry of sanctification is not an easy one. If Gloria and I could not see the results in people's lives, we certainly would be discouraged. Satan comes against sanctification and deliverance ministries harder than any other kinds of ministry for obvious reasons. But—in spite of persecution, even ridicule, being misunderstood by good friends, and attacks on finances—being obedient to Jesus *and* seeing the effects of this ministry in people's lives makes it all worth while.

We agree with author and deliverance minister Win Worley that "casting out evil spirits is a miracle ministry (Mark 9:39) in which results are often instantaneous, spectacular, and lasting."[7] He calls deliverance a "pragmatic" ministry—it works! This ministry is practical in its effect on Christian's lives, and we feel blessed to be entrusted with it.

End Notes

1. Burnie Davis, *How to Have God's Miracle Power in Your life*, (Formerly titled *How to Activate Miracles in Your Life and Ministry*] (Oklahoma: Tulsa, Harrison House, Inc.).
2. "Mud Hut to Modern Miracle," *Full Gospel Business Men's VOICE*, (P. O. Box 5050, Costa Mesa, CA 92628), p. 13.
3. Agnes Sanford. (See Bibliography)
4. Anne White, Winter Park, Florida 32789
5. Dennis and Rita Bennett, Christian Renewal Association, P. O. Box 576, Edmonds, WA 98020.
6. John and Paula Sandford, Elijah House, P. O. Box 722, Coeur d'Alene, Idaho 83814.
7. Win Worley, "Annihilating the Hosts of Hell", *The Battle Royal: Book I* (Indiana: Highland, Hegewisch Baptist Church, 1981), p. 2.

Introduction
Personal Experiences

My first experience with deliverance as part of sanctification came through ministry to two of my five brothers. One had gone to the altar and been "saved" again and again. He could not seem to stay in church or maintain a Christian walk. I had prayed for him many times, and he would last a few days, then fall back again into sin. I began to study the Bible for an understanding of his unstableness, and I found the following scriptures concerning *sanctification:* John 17:17, Romans 15:16, 1 Corinthians 1:30, Ephesians 5:26, 1 Thessalonians 5:23, Hebrews 10:10 and 14, and Hebrews 13:12.

Then I began to look for the hindrances to his living this sanctified life, and God showed me that his past life had allowed evil spirits to gain a hold on him, and they had to be cast out. We took him through the sanctification process, then had him pray the Prayer of Sanctification. (See Chapter 11.) He began to grow in word and in spirit. Today, he is not only still in the church but is a Sunday school teacher.

Another brother was an alcoholic. On many occasions, he had come to me for help, and I had prayed for him to no avail. But the Holy Spirit began to show me some things about why people become addicts. He showed me that as long as a person can exercise his will and stop whatever he is doing wrong, the problem is flesh. But if the person is operating under an obsession, a compulsion, or an addiction, that person is under the authority of a demon. I also had learned that, for deliverance, a person must *want* to be delivered.

Therefore, when my brother called about midnight one night, crying and wanting prayer, *but drunk,* I said, "You have had all day to come to me if you really wanted help. I am not going to minister to you when you are drunk, and I am tired. It would not do you any lasting good, and the devil would just use an apparently "good" deed to steal my time and energy. But *if you are really serious,* come to my house tomorrow at 7 p.m. *sober,* then I will minister to you, and the Lord will set you free." He did, and I did, and the Lord did. Since then my brother has been free.

A Christian Has No Business With a Spirit of Fear

Back in the early Eighties, I went to Belize with some supporters of the late Burnie Davis to intercede in one of his crusades. On the airplane en route from the United States, a pastor and his wife from our group sat across the aisle from me. As soon as we were airborne, the woman grabbed the airsickness bag and began to use it.

I said to myself, "Well, I know what that is, that's a spirit of fear. A Christian ought not to have to put up with that sort of thing. But if I go over there and cast it out of her, they may put me off this plane in a straitjacket. Lord, if you will open a door and make a way, I'll pray for her and get her completely free of that while we are in Belize."

The second morning in Belize it worked out that I was sitting at breakfast around a table with the woman and her hus-

Personal Experiences

band. As we completed a conversation, I looked over at her and said, "You don't have to put up with that thing that's bothering you any longer."

She looked at me and said, "What are you talking about?" (Maybe she thought I was talking about her husband or something!)

I explained that I was talking about the attacks of fear that afflicted her on planes, and she said, "Oh, I have been praying ever since we met you that you would pray for me."

Her husband said, "When can you pray?"

"When do you want me to pray?" I answered and added that we needed a private place so we would not be interrupted.

He said, "We are on our way up to our room. Come on up in a few minutes, and we will have privacy there."

In their room, as I began to talk to them and to pray, the Lord showed me that this spirit of fear had been on her since she was a child. Her mother and father had tried to smother her to death, and that spirit of fear had come into her life then. I told her husband just to stand still and pray in the Spirit. Then I told her to confess fear as sin and to forgive her father and mother.

I commanded that spirit to come out in the name of Jesus, and then asked her if it was gone.

She said, "No, but my head is about to kill me."

While we were talking, her husband kept on praying.

I said, "The headache means it is on its way out. Let's keep praying, and I commanded the spirit and all of its roots to be broken and come out, in the name of Jesus."

After about four more times, I stopped. She began wiping perspiration away and said, "It is gone, thank God, it is gone. It's gone!"

Her husband had an odd look on his face as he said, "I've never had an experience like this before. I don't know if I should tell you or not, you may think I am crazy."

I said, "No, brother. I won't think you are crazy. I have been involved in this a long time, and God said He is going to show me how to get at the root of the problems His people are having. As I learn to get to the root of the problems, He is going to help those people get free of things they have lived with all their lives."

He said, "All right, but what I saw was certainly strange. I saw a tree stump with bushes growing up around it like shoots that come up from a tree that has been cut down. When you began to pray, the stump started to come out of the ground. As you prayed, it would come up a little bit, then a little bit farther. When you quit praying to talk to my wife, it was about half out of the ground. As you began to name different kinds of fear, the shoots began popping loose. Because it wasn't all the way out, I did not stop praying while you talked. When you resumed commanding the demon to go, that stump fell over, turned to a puff of smoke, and disappeared. What did all that mean?"

I said, "For one thing, it shows the devil is a puff of smoke. He does not have power unless we allow him in our lives. But I am not sure about the stump and shoots. Let's ask the Holy Spirit."

So we prayed, and the Holy Spirit told me that this couple knew the Word of God and had bound up the spirit of fear and done everything they had ever been taught. Consequently, the "tree" had been cut down, but the root had not been gotten out. The Holy Spirit said, "I showed you how to get to the root of the problem (the attack by her parents) and get out that root."

The woman said she felt better than she ever had in her life, "so clean and pure and refreshed." Then I gave them some instructions that are good for anyone who has gone through deliverance.

"The Bible says that when spirits are cast out, they go off and wander around in dry places, then say, "I had a good

Personal Experiences

home, and I don't like it out here. Let me go back and see if there is anything in that house. If there isn't, I am moving back in. That means if you get cleaned out and do not fill yourself up with the Word of God, you will get that spirit back and others with it. (Matt. 12:43-45.) If you feel, or even begin to think, this thing might be coming back on you, just say, 'No, you do not belong here. I belong to Jesus.' Then rebuke it in the name of Jesus, tell it to go and leave you alone."

As we waited to board the plane for the return trip, I saw them over in a corner of the airport lounge praying, and he was holding her up. I walked over and asked how they were.

They said, "It was just like you said. As soon as we started talking about getting on the airplane, that fear tried to come back, but we wouldn't let it. We drove it off in the name of Jesus."

On the plane, they got the seats in the tail. Have you ever rode in the tail of a plane? It is not smooth there at the best of times, and in rough weather, those seats can be really uncomfortable. As we came into New Orleans, we hit some weather so rough that without seat belts, we were flipped up out of our seats. I walked back as soon as I could to check on them, and they said, "We have never had a better flight in our lives."

Getting Rid of a Spirit of Suicide

A cousin called me up one day asking for prayer for a friend of hers who was contemplating committing suicide.

She said, "Things aren't going right. His business is failing, and he has had money all his life. Now he can't support his family, and he is planning to kill himself. His wife knows it. Everyone around here knows it because of his actions."

Then she told me of a vision that came to her the night before while she was praying for this man: "In this vision," she said, "I had started up to the church where this man's wife attends to get the pastor to come and pray for the man when Jesus appeared to me.

"Jesus said, 'No, don't go to that church because the pastor does not know how to handle this.'

"So, I said, 'Well, I will get the pastor of my church.'

"Then Jesus said, 'No. He does not know how to handle this man, either.'

"I said, 'Lord, who does know how to handle this situation?'

"And Jesus said, 'Call Jimmy. He can help.' So I am calling you to come up here and pray for this man who is thinking about committing suicide."

I told my cousin I could not just run up to her house and jump on that man and begin praying for him. He did not know anything about deliverance or the kind of praying we do.

I said, "It is hard enough when we pray for Christians!"

"What *can* we do?" she asked.

My suggestion was that she invite this man and his wife for lunch and ask me also, so that I could get acquainted with them and they with me. That would allow the Lord to open a way for me to minister to him. That worked very well, especially since she had already invited them to lunch that very day. When lunch time approached, we all went into the house —but this man. He remained in the yard raking leaves up in a pile and burning trash. He was contemplating how to commit suicide, and his wife was scared. Everyone there was afraid that he was going to slip away, and they were not going to be able to prevent it. And of course, they could not have, if he had really decided to go ahead and take his life.

I said to his wife, "We cannot get him in the house, but don't worry about it. The two of you are one. We will pray a prayer of agreement here, and I will bind up that force in his life. Then he will call me, and I will be able to get him set free."

The people there did not understand all of that, but they were so anxious to see something happen. They began saying, "We agree. We agree," and to feel some reassurance. We

Personal Experiences

prayed together, and two days later, I got a call at noon from the disturbed man wanting help. I went to his house that afternoon and began to share with him the good things from the Word of God in story after story. He could not understand the Bible, not having been in church all of his life. The only way I could share the Word was to give him accounts of things that had happened in our lives and how God met the needs of people, how he healed the sick and raised people up from death beds. After two hours of talking, this man just slid out of his chair onto his knees, looked up at me, and said, "Can you tell me how to get saved?"

I said, "I can if you are ready."

He said, "I am ready," so I led him through Romans 10:9 and 10. Then I took authority over a suicide spirit and a death spirit, and I told the devil to load up everything that he had brought to his man and his household and his business. I spoke as strongly as I knew how and told those evil spirits to haul all of that stuff out of there if it took a train. The power of God came into that house, and it got so hot that people began to look at me wild-eyed. A friend of the man's, a car salesman, turned white as a sheet listening to all this, and pretty soon, he got up and made tracks out of there. He did not want to get too involved! But the man got saved and set free.

That night immediately as he lay down to sleep, a vision of a casket appeared to him with a blackbird pecking around the edge of it—then it vanished. The next he saw was a loaded train. It started off slow then moved faster, and faster, and faster off into the air. He began to worry, however, that he was hallucinating or had gotten himself into "some kind of cult." He had never had an experience like that. So he called me the next morning and related the vision.

He said, "Jimmy, that was the longest train I have seen in my life."

I said, "No, you are not in some kind of cult. Remember that I told the devil yesterday if it took a train to load up all your problems and get them out of your life, to do it? The

Holy Spirit was just showing you that what I had commanded in the name of Jesus was what the demons had done. That was the devil removing a trainload of his oppression from your life."

This experience changed the man's life. He became a Christian and was baptized in the Holy Spirit. We began to pray for his wife, who had been a member of a Baptist church. She had been in and out of bed for almost a year with back problems. God healed her back. After she was baptized in the Holy Spirit, she began almost immediately to move in the revelation gifts. From the day we prayed for him to one year later, he was completely out of debt. His home was saved, he was saved, he and his wife were delivered and healed, and out of debt.

A Baby Gets a Miracle

The acts of God in their own lives made such an impact on that family that not long afterwards, they contacted me about praying for the baby of a friend. The child could not see or hear. Its head was undersized, and the brain was deformed.

I said, "Bring the baby to your house and let me know when I can pray for it. I love to pray for babies. They are so easy to get healed, because they do not have a lot of unbelief and doubt and religious tradition."

When Gloria and I went to their house to pray for the baby, it looked as if everyone in the country had arrived! The house was full of visitors. Praying in a group of unbelievers is hard. You cannot pray with people who do not believe. I am talking about Christian "unbelievers." Real unbelievers are sometimes easier to talk to about healing, deliverance, or miracles than Christians who have been taught those things "are not for today."

I started to leave, but the Holy Spirit spoke to me and said, "Remember what Burnie Davis told you? Change fear to faith, and you can have a miracle."

Personal Experiences

Gloria and I went on into the house then, thinking it was about the best opportunity we would ever have to change fear into faith! Sure enough, inside there were all kinds of fear. The very presence of evil was there. People were all sitting around looking as if we were just coming to supper. I did not want to preach but intended just to pray for the baby and leave, but it did not work out that way. I began to share with them things that had happened in our ministry — and I shared, and I shared, and I shared.

After about forty-five minutes, the Holy Spirit said, "Now it is time. You have turned their faith on, all that are lost as well as all of them that are saved."

I told them we were ready to pray, but I said, "There is one little thing we require. You do not know how to pray in this case, so I do not want you to pray. If you had known how, you would not have brought the child to me. I will do the praying, but you can help me with the prayer. Will you do that?"

They all said they would if they could, and I said, "You can."

I said, "I want you to get a picture in your mind of what that baby would be doing if it was well. See the baby riding a tricycle, playing with a toy, or whatever, just get a picture of the answer instead of the problem."

Then I went around the room asking each person to describe the picture in his or her mind. Each one gave me a different illustration. I asked Gloria and the lady who had invited us to her house to pray in the Spirit while the others held the pictures in their minds and agreed with what I was praying in English.

Two or three different principles were operating in this instance: the principle of agreement, "praying of one mind and one accord"; the principle of looking to the answer, Jesus, instead of the problem, the baby's physical condition; and, the principle of praying in line with the Word of God.

As we began to pray, the Holy Spirit prompted me to go over and lay my hands on the baby's head and speak to its eyes, ears, head, and brain. I commanded the baby *in the name of the Lord Jesus Christ* to be made whole. I commanded the eyes to see, the ears to hear, the head to grow to normal size, and the brain to begin functioning properly. As I finished praying, the baby's grandfather handed the baby to someone else, jumped up, and began pulling off his coat. The power of God had moved in so strong and hot that he could not stand it.

After the parents had taken the child and left, the lady of the house came to me and said, "Does it always happen this way when you pray?"

"It always happens this way when we pray according to the Word," I said. "What, specifically, are you referring to?"

She said, "When you were praying for the baby, Jesus walked out of my kitchen, walked over to where the baby was, and laid His hands on the baby's head."

Jesus always honors His Word. Recently, we were praying in our church, and Jesus appeared there in a vision to several of the people and said, "I enjoy coming here. I love to come here. I go to some churches just to honor My Word, but I love to come here." That is because we praise and worship Him, and we let Him have first place in our intercessory prayer sessions and in our ministry.

The parents had a regular appointment set up with the baby's doctor in three weeks, so during that time, I had them read the Scripture and claim the baby's healing by faith. On the Wednesday night of the appointment, the parents and the grandparents came bursting into our service, full of excitement over what the Lord had done. They were so full of joy they could hardly talk!

The doctor had examined the child, called another doctor for a consultation, then asked them, "What have you been doing to this baby?"

They answered, "Nothing but what you have told us—and praying."

Personal Experiences

He said, "Well, keep up whatever you are doing. It's working. The baby can see and hear. Its head is of normal size, and we can't see anything wrong with it!"

Not too long afterwards, the family moved away from our area, but we have seen the child once since then, and it was still doing fine.

A Heavenly Dentist

One lady saw Jesus walking with me as I moved back and forth. As I laid my hands on people, He would come right with me and lay His hands on people at the same time. Another time, I was praying in our church for a lady who wanted her teeth fixed. They were crooked and out of alignment in her mouth. As I laid hands on her and began to pray, she saw Jesus sitting on the throne in Heaven with His crown on. Whenever I began to pray, she saw Him come down into the pulpit area, walk around the wooden altar and up to where I was. As I laid my hands on her, He laid His hands on her face. Her teeth began to move around in her mouth. The last time I talked with her, she only had one tooth that had not yet moved into its proper place.

She had only been saved a few months, but she began to study the Word and be faithful—and I mean faithful. She began to learn how to submit to authority, and she and her husband both became faithful to the Lord. She had been a cigarette smoker, and one day she went into the bathroom to use whatever preparation she used to clean her teeth, looked into the mirror, and screamed! Her husband came running in, and she said, "Look at my teeth. They are white. Jesus has cleaned my teeth." Jesus will do whatever you allow Him to do, but most of the time, people do not really know who Jesus is."

Faith *as* a Mustard Seed

In addition to Matthew 18:19 (the principle of agreeing in prayer), Matthew 17:20 is a second verse that really set me free. When I was going to Bible school in 1973, this verse helped me understand why I did not get answers to my prayers every time. Most Christians think they know that scripture, and I have heard it taught several different ways. However, the revelation I received personally from the Lord on that verse is what set me free in the area of prayer. The context is the story of a demon the disciples failed to cast out.

> **Then came the disciples to Jesus apart, and said, Why could not we cast him out?**
>
> **And Jesus said unto them: Because of your unbelief: for verily I say to you, If you have faith as a grain of mustard seed, ye shall say unto this mountain, Remove hence to yonder place; and it shall remove: and nothing shall be impossible unto you.**
>
> Matthew 17:19,20

People have said, "If you have faith *the size* of a grain of mustard seed," but the verse does not say *the size of*—it says faith *as* a grain of mustard seed. I wanted to know what a mustard seed believed (its "faith"), so God began to show me. If you have the kind of faith that mustard seed has, it is no problem to believe the Word of God.

The Lord said to me, "Look in Genesis, the first chapter and 26th verse, where I gave man *dominion* over all of the earth, and over everything—every fowl, every creature, everything that creepeth. If man has dominion over that, surely he ought to have faith as a grain of mustard seed."

I said, "What are you talking about, Lord?"

He said, "I called man to have authority here in this earth, and he does not believe Me. I called that mustard seed to do one thing. Now you can take that mustard seed and plant it and say to it, 'Come up turnips, or come up beets,' but what is that seed going to do? It is going to make mustard. It will not come up turnips or beets. It believes what I told it to do and brings that to pass."

Personal Experiences xxxi

God gave man dominion over dualistic creatures, those with only souls and bodies. If your faith is as that mustard seed, you should be able to catch fish when you go fishing—if there are any fish in the water. You should be able to bag the game when you go hunting. If you have cattle, you can pray for them, raise them for beefsteak, or for dairy products, or whatever their purpose is. You have authority over them. Have you ever had problems with roaches? You have authority over everything that creeps. Get rid of them.

You can use Psalm 91 to back up this principle of man's dominion and authority.

I was teaching in a country church once, using Psalm 91. I told the congregation that when we do not know exactly how to pray, we can read Psalm 91 to the problem. This lady spoke up and said they had wasps in the church. When they had Sunday School, the wasps would get stirred up, and they would have to leave the room. They had tried spraying them. They had torn down their nest and done all the things people do to get rid of wasps. After hearing me teach on Psalm 91, they applied the Word to the wasps *in faith,* and they left that building and never came back.

We live in Florida in the middle of fields and once our house became infested with rats in the ceiling. That really annoyed me. Here I was, a man of faith who believed in God, and I had a house full of rats. As I was sitting in my chair studying Psalm 91 in preparation for ministry, I heard them running back and forth over my head.

I said, "Father, I read Psalms 91 to those rats, and I take authority over them."

The rats kept running that night, but the next day I went out into a cornfield next to the house and began to mow. My two Dachshounds began to catch rats. They caught more than thirty that day, and I have never had a rat problem since. There are different ways that you can agree with His Word, but God wants you to learn that He means what He says.

Break the Spirit of Poverty

Most of the time spirits of poverty operate in people's lives in such a way that they do not see demonic influence. They do not see that demons are causing them to speak and act contrary to the Word of God. One day, we were praying with a man who was almost broke.

He said, "We have had a bad time here lately, and I need some financing. I need you to pray for me about my business."

The first thing I asked was, "Are you tithing?" When he said that he was, I began to pray with him. The Lord immediately showed me a vision or revelation or discerning of spirits, whichever you prefer to call it, of an evil spirit standing beside the man. It was a "devouring" spirit. I commanded it to leave him and go—and it would not move. All of us there commanded it to leave and go in the name of the Lord Jesus Christ, and it would not go.

So I said, "Let's just look at that scripture in Malachi that speaks of the devourer and see exactly what it says."

When I turned to Malachi 3:10 and 11, I saw that God said He would rebuke the devourer for the sakes of those who bring the tithes into the storehouse. When we tithe, we do not have to rebuke a devouring spirit. God Himself has said He will do it for us.

I began to pray, "Now, Lord, You said to bring to your remembrance what the Word says, and You said in Your Word that you would rebuke the devourer. Well, there he is now. Are You going to do what You said You would?"

That evil spirit shot out of the house and off that man's property so fast you would have thought a jet had picked him up on the way by. Why? Because God honored His Word. If you operate in His Word, God is going to bring it to pass in your life.

Cleansing Property

Properties—lands and buildings—can be infested with demons just as people can. Some times it is as simple as a curse spoken over the place by a construction worker, words that a demon uses as "legal ground" to stay there and carry out whatever mischief was spoken. Or the curse might come from the land having been forcibly or fraudently taken from its original owners. Perhaps the demon is present because "accursed" items are in the house (Josh. 7:11,12). These items include rock music videos and cassettes or records, occult material, or television programs that loose spirits of lust and/or violence.

A man called us once for a marriage counseling session. He said, "My wife lies all the time. She lies constantly, and I can't stop her. I have done all I know to do, and I want you to talk to her."

We set up an appointment a couple of days later, but the very next day the lady called me saying her husband had left her and she needed help immediately. So Gloria and I rode over to her house about ten miles from where we live. We began to pray and take her through the prayer of sanctification (see Appendix). After some time, we got into an area where we were not making any headway. The lady was saved and filled with the Spirit, and I had bound up all the demons involved—but one was still talking through her. We could not understand it, not having had that problem before. How could this demon be talking through this lady when we had it bound up?

The demon said, "I have lived here a long time, since you were real little, and I'm not leaving!"

Now I do not like a demon to tell me he is not leaving. He does not have a choice, if that person wants to get rid of him. We began to pray and ask the Holy Spirit for revelation and instruction. The Lord showed Gloria a room in that house that was dark. As we continued to pray, He told us that room was the key to a cult spirit.

I asked the woman who she bought the house from. When she told me, I knew the man was an elder in the local Mormon church. Mormons apparently dedicate a room in any of their houses to the ministry of their "god." I do not know all of the ramifications or how it is done, but if whoever buys that house later does not become a Mormon, their marriage goes to pot.

As soon as we knew how to pray, we began to take authority over a spirit of Mormonism and to break the curse that had been placed on the house. We again commanded that spirit to leave, and this time it did. (After that, the woman did not lie anymore.) As we prayed, the Lord showed us that her husband would be returning home. We told her to let us know if he wanted us to minister to him. In just a few days, she called us. As we walked in, he began to tell us about his wife.

I said, "I do not want to hear a word. I want to pray for you first, and when I get through praying, if you want to tell me about your wife, you may."

As we began to pray the Prayer of Sanctification with him, the Lord set him free in every area in which he had problems. Then I asked him what he wanted to tell me about his wife, but then he did not have anything to say. We had gotten rid of all those occult spirits that had been destroying his marriage and his home. In addition, we cut ties to previous marriages. Anytime you do not repent of breaking a vow—even after a divorce—the next marriage will not be stable either. You still have that first vow binding you in a spiritual sense. If you have been through a divorce, repent of not keeping that marriage vow and ask God to forgive you and release you from it.

A Word of Warning to Counselors

Confession for salvation must not only be made with the mouth but must take place in the heart. (Rom. 10:9.10.) With people of some ethnic origin, such as American Indian or Oriental, or with people raised in religious tradition, the confession of faith does not always mean a real change of heart.

Personal Experiences

One man with whom we counseled went through the sanctification process after having been a church goer and professing Christian through his 65th birthday. In sessions with him, the Lord kept showing counselors Jesus outside a door knocking to get in. Finally, one of them asked the man when he was born again, only to find out that he had made a mental commitment and *profession* but had never really received Jesus in his heart.

In the sanctification ministry, it is important to get a witness from the Holy Spirit with every person as to whether he or she has *really* been born again. One of the saddest things to contemplate—next to those who put off receiving Jesus too long—is the plight of those who have been in churches for years, think they are saved, but are not.

PART I
Deliverance and Sanctification

Deliverance and Sanctification

Foundational Principle for Sanctification Ministry

One way to explain why Christians need sanctification is a spiritual principle from the story of Lazarus being raised from the dead. Jesus called his spirit back to life, but then He said to the others standing around, **Loose him and let him go** (John 11:44). After he was loosed, Lazarus would also have had to be cleansed from the grave preparations.

Jesus "raises" our spirits from the death that came upon us through Adam's fall. He does this freely, and we do not have any part in it except to *let* Him do it (to receive it). We cannot earn it, and we do not deserve it.

Our souls and bodies, however, remain bound in the grave wrappings of Satan and the world. Jesus has told ministries in the Body to "loose us and let us go." However, after our spirits have been raised from the dead (salvation), and even after we have been loosed from Satan's bondage (deliverance), we still need cleansing (sanctification).

"Grave preparations" are the things we have accepted, believed, and acted upon from the world's system. That cleansing requires inner healing, healing of memories, pulling up of bitter-root judgments, and pulling down of curses or strongholds. The Bible also speaks of this process as "renewing the mind." (Eph. 4:23, Col. 3:10.) Because we chose through our wills to believe or act upon those things, we have to choose through our wills to discard them, or to allow the Holy Spirit to divide soul from spirit (Heb. 4:12) in order to give us a new heart.

Unless our souls are cleansed through *present sanctification*, God's vessels are hindered from total obedience and faithfulness. If this goes on long enough in enough people, the Church becomes stagnant or lukewarm. So many Christians of John Wesley's day were nominal or lukewarm that the Holy Spirit had to bring a major wave of emphasis on cleansing (sanctification) to get the Body of Christ moving again. The same thing has happened in this century.

1
Why Do Christians Need Sanctification?

Sanctification, according to most Bible scholars, is three-fold: past, present, and future:[1]

Sanctification is past, or already done in us, when we are born again. New spirits are given to us immediately upon receiving Jesus as Savior.

Sanctification is present because the soul (mind, will, and emotions) is cleansed progressively (Phil. 3:12-14, Col. 3:10) as we allow God to renew our minds, deny our wills in favor of His, and bring our emotions in line with Jesus to display the fruit of the Spirit (Gal. 5:22).

Sanctification is future because our bodies will not be sanctified until we receive new transfigured bodies at the resurrection. (Rom. 8:11.)

In order to participate in God's process of ongoing sanctification, we must allow the old nature to be changed to conform to the new spirit. The Holy Spirit immediately occupies the spirit of one born again, because he has been given through the grace of God a "new wineskin" made without spot or blemish.

The Holy Spirit, however, cannot usually be fully housed in the old container of the soul. There are "cracks" (wounds) or "holes" (things that give place to the devil) in the soul (mind, will, and emotions—personality) that allow the old nature to remain, at least indirectly, under the authority of Satan. What warfare goes on inside people in this condition! This is why so many Christians never seem to maintain a victorious life, in spite of revelation knowledge about faith, the power of the tongue, a prayer language, and the Holy Spirit in manifestation of gifts.

Hindrances to Sanctification: Doctrines of Man

One hindrance to sanctification for evangelical-fundamentalists is the doctrine that God does everything He wants to do in one operation: salvation. They believe if you have problems after that, you were never really saved, or "God wants to teach you a lesson."

On the other hand, a hindrance to Charismatic-Pentecostal Christians is the doctrine that baptism in the Holy Spirit does everything that needs doing!

Being "filled with the Holy Spirit" empowers Christians —it does not clean them up. The *baptism of the Holy Spirit* is for the purposes of ministering to the Body and for involvement in spiritual warfare. *Sanctification* is the process of perfecting the saints. One move of the Holy Spirit (baptism) is to enable a believer to minister to others and prevail against the gates of hell (Mat. 16:18); the other move (sanctification) is to clean up the individual believer.

You cannot have a new (renewed or restored) soul without the Holy Spirit. But because of man's free will, the Holy Spirit—even through the process of baptism—must flow through man's soul as the water of a river flows around obstacles in its path. To have a clear channel, engineers must dredge out the depths and clear out all the debris. To have a

Why Do Christians Need Sanctification?

clear channel through a believer, the Holy Spirit must operate through the believer's submission and commitment of will to dredge out the depths of slime and dirt in the soul and to clean out soulish, carnal debris.

We are not "limiting" the Holy Spirit, but illustrating God's primary principle in dealing with man: He will only do what each person through a free will and free choices will allow Him to do. God's desire is for all to be saved, but all are not— only those who choose. *God desires for all of His children to be freed of bondage and cleansed, but all are not—only those who will receive deliverance and sanctification.*

The biggest hindrance to sanctification and deliverance, of course, is a belief that the devil either does not operate very much today or that he cannot bother Christians.

Yet another hindrance is the doctrine from Greek philosophy that man is dualistic—soul and body, not spirit, soul, and body. The New Testament uses different Greek words for spirit and soul (in Greek, *pneuma* means "spirit" and *psuche* means "soul") and never uses "spirit" and "soul" synonymously, but many people—even scholars—still do not believe that man *is* a spirit who *has* a soul and *lives in* a body.

If *spirit* and *soul* are the same, Jesus and Paul disagreed with one another: Jesus talked of being born again as a onetime experience, and Paul spoke of salvation as "progressive." (Phil. 3:12-16, 2 Cor. 4:16.) But if Jesus was talking about the basic process of becoming a new creature, part of a new race through being given a new spirit, and Paul was talking about the progressive process of sanctification of the soul to the image of Christ, then there is no contradiction.

A major cause of unbelief concerning ministries of healing and deliverance is the doctrine that the Old Testament does not apply to us (yet the proponents of this doctrine use many Old Testament verses in their prophecy scenarios). The erroneous idea that Jesus came to do away with the writings of the Old Testament was around even when He was on earth. Many believe that "we are not under law, but grace," and overlook Jesus' words to those who thought His teachings did away with what we know as the Old Testament:

> **Think not that I am come to destroy the law, or the prophets: I am not come to destroy, but to fulfil.**
>
> **For verily I say unto you, till heaven and earth pass, one jot or one tittle shall in no wise pass from the law, till all be fulfilled.**
> **Matthew 5:17,18**

Through Jesus' shedding of His blood on the cross, we no longer have the law written on tablets and enforced as a teacher or taskmaster, but we have His law (the same commandments) written on our hearts (our consciences) by the Holy Spirit. Paul explained this to the Galatian church. Under the law, God's people were as minor children. Paul wrote:

> **The heir, as long as he is a child, differeth nothing from a servant, though he be lord of all.**
>
> **Wherefore thou art no more a servant, but a son.**
> **Galatians 4:1,7**

More is expected of a grown son than of a servant or of a child. The law written on our hearts and the indwelling of the Holy Spirit require *more* obedience (living by the *spirit* as well as the *letter* of the law) and greater sanctification than was required of the Israelites. Israel had the law as an *outer discipline* to keep them in line with God's ways. We are to live by an *inner discipline* that is not possible when our natural and spiritual selves war against each other.

The Bible also says that Jesus never changes (Heb. 13:8), which means that God never changes, and that means the principles or laws of God that we see worked out in the Old

Why Do Christians Need Sanctification?

Testament have never changed and will not change in the future. The only parts of the Old Testament not applicable to us are the religious and civil statutes. The religious rituals of sacrifice and offerings involved in Temple worship were fulfilled on the cross and are memorialized in our sacrament of the Last Supper. The Holy Spirit dwelled on earth in the Ark of the Covenant, the Holy of Holies of the Temple. Today, He lives in our spirits. But nothing about the way we are to live (the Law)—obedient, faithful, and holy or sanctified—has changed.

Paul wrote in 1 Corinthians 10:11 that all of the things in the Old Testament were examples for us and were written down for the admonition, or teaching, of those **upon whom the ends of the world are come;** in other words, for all those born since Jesus ascended into heaven. An *example* means "something (especially conduct) that is worthy of imitation."[2] If the Old Testament had been "done away with," we would not be told to use it as an example. His principles (laws) have never changed and never will.

The "Curse of the Law"

Those who quote Paul's letter to the Galatians, **Christ hath redeemed us from the curse of the law** (Gal. 3:13) as proof that the curses of the Old Testament are no longer valid are missing the point of Paul's letter. There are three kinds of curses mentioned in the Bible: the curse of death (separation from the life of God) as a *penalty* on all mankind for Adam's sin, the "blessings and curses" that are covenant promises for hearing and obeying or rebelling and not obeying God, and the curse of the law.

Jesus became a curse for us by hanging on a tree (Gal. 3:13) and blotted out the *penalty* of death against us. However, for that to be effective, it must be appropriated by faith. Then God gives us new spirits as free gifts because we are not responsible for Adam's sin, although we inherited the penalty.

The "blessings and curses" of the Abrahamic covenant (that continue under the new covenant—see chapter 4) affect the quality of our life on earth and primarily involve the soul and body. Freedom from those curses and the right to the blessings also was bought for us on the cross; but, *just as a new spirit must be received,* freedom from curses must be received *in the soul and body.* Walking in faith for one's finances and health is a receiving of freedom from the curse of poverty and sickness, for example. This sort of freedom is progressive, *present sanctification.*

Paul was not talking about freedom from the penalty of Adam's sin nor about blessings and curses. He was talking about continuing to try to justify (save) oneself by works. The "curse of the law" is *the attempt to be saved by keeping the law rather than through Jesus.*

Paul wrote, "Did you receive the Holy Spirit through good works of keeping the law or through the hearing of faith?" (Gal. 3:2.) Paraphrase.

Paul was saying, "We keep the law of God *because* we are His children, but we cannot *become* His children by keeping the law."

James did not write that being free *from the curse of the law* meant being free from obeying the laws of God. He wrote:

> **Brothers, do not slander one another. Anyone who speaks against his brother or judges him, speaks *against the law* and judges it.**
>
> **When you judge the law, you are not *keeping* it, but *sitting in judgment* on it.**
>
> **There is only one Lawgiver and Judge, the one who is able to save and destroy. But you—who are you to judge your neighbor?**
>
> **James 4:11-13 NIV**

Why Do Christians Need Sanctification? 11

Those who throw out the Old Testament for Christians are *sitting in judgment* on it. An extreme application of that doctrine is "relativism," the philosophy that each person can decide for himself what is right or wrong in a given situation. Jesus answered His critics this way:

> . . . Why do ye also transgress the commandment of God by your tradition?
>
> Matthew 15:3

> But in vain do they worship me, *teaching for doctrines the commandments of men.*
>
> Matthew 15:9

These Things Are Not for Today

In our day, the various religious doctrines and teachings that mix man's wisdom with the Word (traditions) are what Jesus is trying to get us to give up—not His laws. One example of the "traditions" of our day that hinder sanctification and the healing and restoration of spirit, soul, and body is the doctrine that signs and wonders and the gifts of the Holy Spirit stopped when the last apostle died. That doctrine contradicts the Word which says that God never changes (Heb. 13:8).

That doctrine originated with religious leaders of the past few hundred years who attempted to justify with man's wisdom the fact that they saw no miracles or supernatural events occurring in the Church. Instead of returning to the Word and then researching the history of the Church to find where it left God's ways, *they went looking for an excuse for the Church.* Instead of defending God by seeking His truth, they defended the Church—and developed a false doctrine.

Many of those who believe the Old Testament is not for today continue to take away from the Scripture by saying part of the New Testament is not for us either: prophets and apostles, signs and wonders, and the manifestations of the Holy Spirit. These people teach and believe that everything today from speaking in tongues to casting out demons is of the devil.

Jesus answered similar critics by asking, "Can a house divided against itself stand?" (Mk. 3:24-26.) Will Satan cast out his own followers? Certainly not. There have been a few instances where demons have faked deliverance, but others immediately moved in so that the state of the person "delivered" was worse than at first.[3] Counterfeit deliverance is uncommon and occurs only when no one with discernment of spirits is in authority.

Christians Need Cleansing From "Grave Preparations"

One way to explain why Christians need sanctification is a spiritual principle from the story of Lazarus being raised from the dead. Jesus called his spirit back to life, but then He said to the others standing around, **Loose him and let him go** (John 11:44). After he was loosed, Lazarus would also have had to be cleansed from the grave preparations.

Jesus "raises" our spirits from the death that came upon us through Adam's fall. He does this freely, and we do not have any part in it except to *let* Him do it (to receive it). We cannot earn it, and we do not deserve it.

Our souls and bodies, however, remain bound in the grave wrappings of Satan and the world. Jesus has told ministries in the Body to "loose us and let us go." However, after our spirits have been raised from the dead (salvation), and even after we have been loosed from Satan's bondage (deliverance), we still need cleansing (sanctification).

"Grave preparations" are the things we have accepted, believed, and acted upon from the world's system. That cleansing requires inner healing, healing of memories, pulling up

Why Do Christians Need Sanctification?

of bitter-root judgments, and pulling down of curses or strongholds. The Bible also speaks of this process as "renewing the mind." (Eph. 4:23, Col. 3:10.) Because we chose through our wills to believe or act upon those things, we have to choose through our wills to discard them, or to allow the Holy Spirit to divide soul from spirit (Heb. 4:12) in order to give us a new heart.

Unless our souls are cleansed through *present sanctification*, God's vessels are hindered from total obedience and faithfulness. If this goes on long enough in enough people, the Church becomes stagnant or lukewarm. So many Christians of John Wesley's day were nominal or lukewarm that the Holy Spirit had to bring a major wave of emphasis on cleansing (sanctification) to get the Body of Christ moving again. The same thing has happened in this century.

Howard Pittman of Foxworth, Mississippi, a man who was allowed to visit Heaven and see the hierarchy of demons operating in the Second Heaven during a 1979 death experience, says everything God commissioned him to come back and tell can be summed up in one message: holiness (sanctification). He wrote:

> For those who call themselves Christian, this is the Laodicean Church age in which we live. A high majority of Christians are, in fact, living deceived lives. They talk Jesus and play church, but do not live it. They claim to be Christians and live like the devil. They have bought the great lie of Satan that they are alright. . . . As far as their Christian lives are concerned, they believe they are comfortable and have need of nothing, and as a result, they are only lukewarm Christians—if Christians at all![4]

Much of the Church seems trapped in soul-living like a man caught in a swamp who keeps moving his feet and not going anywhere. Getting rid of the mud of the world would allow the Body to move onto solid ground. I believe the present move of the Holy Spirit is a move of sanctification, or a return to Christian lifestyles based on the holiness of God. Christians who want to be part of this move should begin to study and research sanctification, to pray more for insight and guidance concerning their own lives, and to seek deliverance. God historically has come to clean up His people, to warn them, before He judges them—and He judges His people before He judges the world. (1 Pet. 4:17.)

One word of caution: We must be careful not to allow the devil to push us to the other extreme from "cheap grace," which is Pharisaism. We must not concentrate on cleaning the outward appearance and inwardly remain "whited sepulchres" (Matt. 23:25,26), those who look alive but are relying on dead works of the soul. Also, we must not judge others while overlooking our own faults. (Matt. 7:3-5; Luke 6:41,42.) The secular world—and many in the Church—have reacted in self-righteousness to this move of the Spirit, not in true righteousness.

End Notes

1. *Five Views on Sanctification* (Michigan: Grand Rapids, Academie Books, Copyright (c) 1987).
2. *Oxford American Dictionary* (New York: Oxford University Press, 1980), p. 222, Definition 2.
3. The Challenging Counterfeit, by Raphael Gasson (Plainfield, New Jersey: Logos International, 1966.)
4. Howard Pittman, *Demons: An Eyewitness Account* (no publisher or date listed), p. 93.

2
"Holes" and "Cracks" in the Wineskin of the Soul

Areas in which Christians *need* sanctification because of being born into and living under a satanic world order include:

Hurts and wounds caused by past sins; hurts and wounds caused by inherited consequences of ancestral sins; hurts and wounds caused by other people; bitter-root judgments and expectancies; rejection by oneself and others; bindings in one's life through negative words, prayers, and confessions, or words spoken, by oneself and others; attacks by **principalities, powers, rulers of darkness, wicked spirits in high places** (Eph. 6:12); rebellion against those in authority—parents, school officials, police, pastors, government leaders, husbands, or employers; performance orientation, and ungodly soul ties. Some of these things are self-evident. Others require a word of explanation.

A. *Hurts and wounds caused by our sins.*

The head-knowledge of forgiveness does not automatically replace old programs in the subconscious, the control-center of our behavior. Pastor Casey Treat of Seattle, Washington, uses what we think are very graphic terms to explain this. He calls the *conscious* mind the "judgemind" and the *subconscious* the "robotmind." The robot controls behavior, not the judge. The judgemind simply deals with taking in new data and forming opinions. It has *no control* over behavior, which is why so many people can believe one thing and do another.[1]

Each time we sinned against God by breaking His spiritual laws, even before becoming His children, we hurt ourselves. We made wounds in ourselves by the actual sins and more wounds by the aftereffects of remorse, guilt, and pain. Also, there usually have been further, deeper hurts left by the consequences of those sins. John Sandford wrote in *The Transformation of the Inner Man:*

> Rightly grasping that every sinful deed was fully washed away, the Body *failed to realize that every part of the heart had not fully appropriated the good news of that fact.* Rightly believing that positionally the old man is fully dead and a totally new creature is present, the Body failed to grasp that in fact many areas of the inner man have refused even to be seen, much less to lie down and accept that death. So Christians proclaimed, "I'm born anew; I'm a totally changed man; I'm a new creature; the past is all gone," while the testimony of their lives all too often proclaimed the opposite. And the good news of Jesus was blasphemed to unbelievers. *Healing of the inner man seemed to these believers a denial of their salvation, and still does to many today.*[2]

Hurts and wounds of the spirit and soul are not "psychological" problems but as real as physical hurts and wounds. Following are a few things that cause hurts and wounds:

—Dishonoring parents (Eph. 6:1-3, Deut. 5:16, Prov. 20:20).

"Holes" and "Cracks" in the Wineskin of the Soul

—Occult, or Cult, involvement (to be discussed at greater length in later chapters).
—Fornication (Acts 15:20; 1 Cor. 5:1, 6:13; Eph. 5:3; 1 Tim. 4:3; Rev. 14:8).
—Transgression of any law of God.

> **For he that said, Do not commit adultery, said also, Do not kill. Now if thou commit no adultery, yet if thou kill, thou art become a transgressor of the law.**
> **James 2:11**

Jesus even took this principle further. He said, "If you do not kill, yet you hate your "brother," you are a transgressor of the law." (Matt. 5:21,22.)

When you are born again, you receive forgiveness of your sins. God removes them **as far as the east is from the west** (Ps. 103:12), but they are not automatically removed from your consciousness. In the sight of God, *positionally*, you are washed whiter than snow (Isa. 1:18), but in your own inner sight (subconscious) the marks left by those sins are still there. The "judgemind" knows better, but the "robotmind" controls your behavior and attitudes to yourself and others. The subconscious (the control room of the old nature) must be sanctified, or renewed to conform to the new spirit.

Particularly if they stem from attitudes and habits formed in your childhood, consequences—or even the sins themselves—keep cropping up in your life. A born again person may get drunk, or lose his temper, or fall into pride again and again. His salvation is intact, because *works did not get him saved and works will not lose him his salvation*—only his free will to receive or reject Jesus can do that. That person may repent over and over, but the harvest of that seed planted long ago will continue. The ax must be laid to the root of the tree (Matt. 3:10) for it to cease growing fruit.

You *cannot* erase the memory of past sins from your life as if certain events never happened, but the continuing harvest of those sins can be eliminated through sanctification and/or deliverance. The memories are healed through sanctification, so the problems do not reoccur. Then seeds of love and obedience and faithfulness to God and His principles (laws)can be planted in order for the fruit you reap to be that of the Holy Spirit. (Gal. 5:22.)

B. *Inherited consequences of hurts and wounds caused by ancestral sins.*

These include negative emotions such as "stubbornness, anger and temper, argumentativeness, nervousness, tension, mental disorders, fears of various kinds, and so forth; sickness and disease such as diabetes and low blood sugar, heart disease, high blood pressure, strokes, cancer, arthritis, migraine headaches, and many others (I believe sickness almost always is a direct result of an evil spirit or spirits); curses, hexes, and witchcraft; drug addiction and alcoholism; and racial traits. Following are some examples of inherited racial traits from which we need to be delivered or from which we need to have ties from the past broken:

—American Indian (idolatry, addictions to hunting, fishing, nature worship, sexual perversions, divorce and home wrecking, self-abasement, stoicism, white and black magic and superstitions, encantations, prejudice, witchcraft and medicine men, destruction, recklessness, and murder).

—Irish (superstitions, fantasies, vivid imaginations, imaginary playmates, the "luck of the Irish," alcoholism, temper and anger, traditionalism).

—English or Anglo-Saxon (stoicism, idolatry, witchcraft, superstitions, suppressed emotions, tendency toward nagging).

—African (witch doctors, voodoo, black and white magic, idolatry, fear, cannibalism, prejudice, encantations, chants, dancing, revolution and recklessness).

—Italian (idolatry, strong Jezebelic and control personalities, alcoholism, poverty, and necromancy).

C. *Hurts and wounds caused by others.*

The deepest hurts are those we receive from family and friends, intentional or unintentional. Christians are not exempt from these wounds and need healing in these areas as much as in the physical. These include hurts from parents, spouses, or children; friends or peers in childhood and as adults; pastors or spiritual leaders; rejection or violence, such as child abuse, rape or incest; embarrassing events; grievous disappointments; divorce and related consequences such as adoption, foster homes, and broken homes; and even gossip. **The words of a talebearer are as wounds, and they go down into the innermost parts of the belly** (Prov. 18:8, 26:22).

D. *Bitter-Root Judgments and Expectancies.*

> **See to it that no one comes short of the grace of God; that no *root of bitterness* springing up causes trouble, and by it many be defiled.** Paraphrase.
> **Heb. 12:15**

This consequence might also be called "sowing and reaping." (Gal. 6:7.) God does not have one law for the natural and one for the spiritual. The spiritual law of reaping what is sown is expressed in physics as the law of "equal and opposite reaction for every action" and in chemistry as "every formula or equation must balance." The law of God is expressed differently in each field of life.

> These three simple laws affect all life: 1) Life will go well for us in every area in which we could in fact honor our parents and life will not go well in every area in which we could not honor them; 2) We will receive harm in the same

areas of life in which we have meted out judgment against others; 3) We will most surely reap what we have sown.[3]

Also, when you plant one seed, you do not get just one seed back. The law of sowing and reaping means that one seed may bring an abundant harvest. Sanctification enables the Holy Spirit to pull up "bad seeds" in Christians' lives and stop the harvest of bad fruit.

E. *Performance orientation.*

People with this "grave-wrapping" are bound by the need to be perfect, the unconscious motivation that only through their works will they be loved. In Christians, many times this problem involves a religious spirit (demon). They may seem to be the best workers in the church or the best housekeepers, but their motives are not out of love of God and their families but out of a fear that they will never be "good enough." They are back under the "curse of the law." In a sense, they have become their own "gods." It takes sanctification-deliverance to believe that God's grace is *undeserved, unmerited favor.*

F. *Ungodly soul ties.*

Soul ties can be mental or emotional. "Ungodly soul ties" can exist with parents, with partners in illicit relationships or sometimes even in marriage relationships, with friends in the form of spiritually adulterous relationships, or through an attitude of idolatry toward a Christian leader. *Ungodly soul ties* involve "cleaving to" or "being bound to" any person or thing or place through negative, perverse, or misplaced emotions.

Since *sanctification* (cleansing) is not possible until the resurrected person has been unbound, most people need deliverance in order to become free of the wrong kind of soul ties. But one major point in fundamentalist, evangelical, and even

"Holes" and "Cracks" in the Wineskin of the Soul

Pentecostal-Charismatic theology for the past one hundred years has been that Christians cannot have demons! If Christians cannot have demons, then they are not truly "bound," are they? They should be free as soon as they are saved. Then why are so many with new, recreated spirits still bound up? The answer is in 2 Peter 2:19: . . . **For a man is a slave to whatever has mastered him.** The truth is that many Christians *are* still bound by Satan and by soul problems.

End Notes

1. Casey Treat, *Living a Transformed Life* (Oklahoma: Tulsa, Harrison House Inc. Copyright (c) 1987 by Casey Treat Ministries, Seattle, Washington).
2. John and Paul Sandford, *The Transformation of the Inner Man* (New Jersey: South Plainfield, Bridge Publishing, Inc.), p. 6,7.
3. Ibid., p. 239, 242.

3
Can a Christian Have an Evil Spirit?

Instead of confining casting out of demons to sinners, the Bible teaches it the other way around. We should not be casting evil spirits out of unbelievers. A person who has not been born again into the Body of Christ would only receive more evil spirits and be worse off than before! (Luke 11:24-26.)

Frank Hammond, well-known Texas minister and author, says:

> I see no ground for administering deliverance to an unbeliever other than a direct word from the Lord. Only God knows the future and whether he would accept Christ as his Savior. . . . Deliverance is not a game. It is serious business. It is for those who mean business with God. The question, then, is not CAN a non-Christian be delivered, but SHOULD he be delivered? Normally, his spirit should be delivered first, and that is by the new birth.[1]

According to Jesus, children of God are the only people who have a *right* to be set free from evil spirits (Mark 7:25-30).

Jesus called deliverance **the children's bread** in Mark 7:27. No Bible-based deliverance ministry casts out demons unless the person is born again, or unless conversion takes place immediately after deliverance.

Looking at Jesus' ministry, we see that most of those from whom he cast out demons were not sinners but believing Jews. One of Jesus' own disciples, those who were closest to Him, allowed Satan to enter into him. (Lk. 22:3.) Judas had been a trusted follower, even handling the money. Many of Jesus' healings of God's people involved casting out evil spirits. (Mat. 17:18 NIV; Luke 6:18.)

Some might say, "Yes, but Jesus had not yet gone to the cross. None of the people to whom he ministered were born again. None of them had the Holy Spirit dwelling within."

What about Ananias and Sapphira? They were included in **the multitude of them that believed and had all things in common** (Acts 4:32). Peter said to Ananias, **Why hath** *Satan filled thine heart* **to** lie to the Holy Ghost, and to keep back part of the price of the land? (Acts 5:3). The context makes it plain that Ananias *and* Sapphira were not only born again but *filled with the Holy Spirit*. Peter certainly behaved as if they were bonafide believers and members of the community. Peter did not say they were *filled with Satan* but that they had allowed Satan *to fill them with a lie.*

Peter did not say, "Well, what can you expect? They were not really born again."

On the other hand, Elymas the sorcerer was called a **child of the devil** in Acts 13:10, and the seven sons of Sceva, a Jewish chief priest, were called **vagabond Jews, exorcists.** Obviously none of these eight men were born again. (Acts 19:13-20.) They attempted to use the name of Jesus, *whose authority had been given only to those who believe on Him* (Matt. 28:18-20; John 20:23; 2 Cor. 10:8), and were soundly beaten by the demons who knew they were not authorized to use that name. The distinction between believers who allowed the devil to influence them and people who were not believers

Can a Christian Have an Evil Spirit?

but had dealings with the devil is pretty clear in most passages in the New Testament.

Paul wrote the assembly at Ephesus, **Neither give place to the devil** (Eph. 4:27). *The Amplified Bible* puts it this way:

> **Leave no [such] room or foothold for the devil—give no opportunity to him.**

Paul was writing to *born again people* about **putting on the new man** (Eph. 4:24). If there was no possibility of their being demon-influenced or oppressed and if there was no continuing process of sanctification, Paul would not have bothered to write in this way. They had *become* new men. He was trying to show them how to live like new men. He addressed both satanic bondage and the cleansing process in Ephesians 4. Then in chapter 6, he warned them to **stand against the wiles** (in Greek, *methodeia,* meaning "methodical pursuit") **of the devil** (v. 11). Paul went on to specifically name the enemy.

> **For we wrestle not against flesh and blood, but against principalities, against powers, against the rulers of the darkness of this world, against spiritual wickedness in high places.**
> **Ephesians 6:12**

Noted author and minister Don Basham wrote in one of his books:

> The fact that one is a Christian does not assure that every area of his life is free from demonic bondage. A Christian can be tormented or afflicted by evil spirits in some area of his life and still be a sincere Christian; just as he can be tormented by physical illness (which is also from Satan) and still be a sincere Christian.[2]

Basham points out that objections to deliverance ministries many times are really fear of demons, prejudice, ignorance, or simply man's critical nature. He said, "Man is prone to criticize those whose beliefs and practices differ from his own. This is shown even in the Scriptures themselves,"[3] and he mentioned the Jewish Christians' disbelief in Paul's ministry to the Gentiles. (Acts 15:1,2.)

More New Testament References to Demons and Christians

Other New Testament writings also warn about demons influencing, afflicting, or oppressing Christians. In 2 Corinthians 11:3,4, Paul is concerned about the Christians receiving a different (Greek: *heteros,* meaning "of a different kind") spirit than the Holy Spirit, or another Jesus, or another gospel. He wrote to the Galatians with great concern that they would turn back to the *elemental spirits* (demons) whose slaves *they once were.* (Gal. 4:9 RSV.)

Peter did not write to sinners about being "devoured" by Satan, but to believers.

> **Be sober, be vigilant, because your adversary the devil, as a roaring lion, walketh about,** *seeking whom he may devour;* **whom resist stedfast in the faith.**
> **1 Peter 5:8,9**

Satan is not seeking to devour people *whom he already has.*

> **Submit yourselves therefore unto God.** *Resist* **Satan and he shall flee from you.**
> **James 4:7**

Why would Christians be admonished to **resist Satan,** if he could have no effect on them?

Results of Unbelief in Deliverance

Several false teachings are perpetuated by the "erroneous and unscriptural position that believers cannot have demons."[4] Some of these are:

Can a Christian Have an Evil Spirit? 27

—Everything is attributed to "the flesh."
—All problems are due to the "lack of surrender," in other words, these people's salvation is not real.
—People are left open to be snared into cults by angels of light.
—Demons are given legal ground to stay.
—Spiritual pride afflicts many religious leaders. Not believing in demonic oppression, they accept that demon of pride as part of themselves.
—Despair and hopelessness are fostered within the demonized.

Deliverance minister Win Worley says:

> Deliverance will increasingly assume critical importance in the days ahead as God moves to purge and cleanse the Church. Believers will never be able to function to *full capacity* in witnessing, holy living, warfare, or the operation of the gifts of the Holy Spirit so long as the devil has this stranglehold through his deadly fifth column *within* them.[5]

Dr. Merrill F. Unger, noted author and former professor at Dallas Theological Seminary, wrote in one of his books:

> Since fallen man is unable to keep God's moral law perfectly, and is acceptable to God only on the basis of Christ's atonement, all men, saved as well as unsaved, can be subjected to demon influence.
> In demon influence, evil spirits exert power over a person short of actual possession. Such influence may vary from mild harassment to extreme subjection when body and mind become dominated and held in slavery by spirit agents. *Christians, as well as non-Christians, can be so influenced.* They may be oppressed, vexed, depressed, hindered, and bound by demons.
> Even in evangelical circles, where Satan and demons are recognized as existing, an atmosphere of make-believe

prevails with regard to the extensive influence these malevolent spirits exercise against the human race. Though tacitly, the unscriptural idea is widely entertained that demonism presents no serious threat to the Christian today . . . the intensity of spiritual conflict and the disastrous results of defeat are little recognized, and many believers fall victim to Satan because they are not aware of his presence![6]

It is easy to see that the most serious consequence of the erroneous belief that demons cannot affect Christians is that millions live defeated lives, therefore God's plan to totally destroy the works of the devil—which the Bible says was Jesus' primary reason for coming to earth (1 John 3:8)—is slowed down.

In addition to unrepented sins or sins whose roots have not been "axed" (negative emotions), Christians can be plagued with demons through generational sin, through curses coming from their own or others' words, or through personal involvement in occult things.[7] We will discuss these in the next chapters.

End Notes

1. Hammond, Frank and Ida Mae, *Pigs in the Parlor* (Missouri: Kirkwood, Impact Books, 1973), p. 138.
2. Don Basham, *Can a Christian Have a Demon?* (Pennsylvania: Monroeville, Whitaker Books, 1971), p. 61.
3. Ibid., p. 27.
4. Worley, p. 9.
5. Ibid., p. 7.
6. Merrill F. Unger, *Demons in the World Today* (Illinois: Wheaton, Tyndale House Publishers, 1971; Twelfth Printing, 1982), pp. 116, 113, 188.
7. Ernest Gruen, *Freedom to Choose,* Pittsburgh and Colfax Streets, Springdale, Pennsylvania 15144.

4
The Curse Causeless Shall Not Come

Two root causes of curses connected with the covenant are found in God's Word. They are: 1) not *listening* to the voice (Word) of God, and 2) not *obeying* the voice (Word) of God. On the other hand the two root causes of blessings are the same things: *listening and obeying!*

> **And it shall come to pass,** *if thou shalt hearken* **diligently unto the voice of the Lord thy God, to observe and to do all his commandments which I command thee this day, that the Lord thy God will set thee on high above all the nations of the earth.**
> **But it shall come to pass, if thou will** *not* **hearken unto the voice of the Lord thy God, to observe to do all his commandments and his statutes which I command thee this day; that all these curses shall come upon thee, and overtake thee.**
> **Deuteronomy 28:1,2,15**

> If ye be *willing and obedient,* ye shall eat the good of the land.
> But if ye *refuse and rebel,* ye shall be devoured with the sword: for the mouth of the Lord hath spoken it.
> Isaiah 1:19,20

The *Oxford American Dictionary*[1] says a *curse* is: 1. a call for evil to come upon a person or thing (and) 2. the evil produced by this. It also says *be cursed with* means "to have as a burden or source of harm." Being freed from the curse of death and from the curse of the law by getting new spirits as free gifts through God's mercy does not eliminate the curse for not hearing and obeying. New spirits still have old programs which cause the same old things to happen.

Old Things Happen to New Creations

We are freed from the *penalty* of sin when we become born again, but we are not automatically freed from the *consequences* of disobedience to God, listed as curses in the Bible. Most Charismatics accept the truth that there is a curse, or a consequence, of poverty on those who do not tithe. Well, that is Old Testament! You find it in Malachi 3:8-11. It is inconsistent to accept one Old Testament curse as truth for today and not the others.

We may be "new creations" in Christ (2 Cor. 5:17), but in this world, old things still have their effects or consequences, and *old things still happen to new creations.* So we need help in getting rid of those old things and in repenting and renouncing things of the past that might result in the devil having a legal right to bring cursed conditions on us. We must *receive* God's dividing of the soul and spirit (Heb. 4:12) in order to have a new (sanctified) soul—just as we must *receive* salvation in order to obtain a new spirit. The *penalty* for the unbelief of the Israelites who feared to take the Promised Land was being forbidden to enter. The *consequences* of the penalty was forty years in the wilderness. Hebrews 3:19 NIV says:

So we see that they were not able to enter, because of unbelief.

The penalty for a young woman who committed fornication or adultery in Old Testament days would have been death, and in more modern times, being ostracized from "good" society if her sin became known. Today, no one is stoned for sexual sins or very much condemned. *The penalty has been done away with.* But the consequences remain—ranging from having an illegitimate child to various sexual diseases, even AIDS. The *penalty* for breaking God's law was paid by Jesus, but the *consequences*—the curses of the Old Testament—remain as poverty, or sickness, or mental and emotional problems.

The root cause of curses, or consequences, may be personal, generational, or environmental—the "spiritual dirt" from the secular world system (society) and the times in which we live. Although we have been born into the Kingdom of God, without sanctification our lives are affected by Satan through *consequences*—not penalties—of past actions and attitudes rooted in his kingdom.

> **In whom the *god of this world* hath blinded the minds of them which believe not, lest the light of the glorious gospel of Christ, who is the image of God, should shine unto them.**
>
> **2 Corinthians 4:4**

Gloria and I cannot emphasize too much that we are not a "ministry of works." In Galatians, Paul wrote that anyone who attempts to justify himself by works (keeping the law outwardly) and not by faith in Jesus' atonement remains under the *curse of the law.* (Gal. 3:10-14.)
• We are not saved by works but by faith.
• We are not healed by works but by faith.
• We are not sanctified by works but by faith.

- We are not delivered from cursings unto blessings by works but by faith.

Why Old Testament Curses Still Affect Believers

In addition to the distinction between penalties and consequences and the difference between receiving a new spirit through God's mercy *and* a renewed soul through God's mercy and our cooperation, two more aspects need to be discussed. They are *time required for fulfillment* and the fact that consequences are conditions of the Abrahamic covenant and not directly tied to the fall of Adam.

If Jesus accomplished all freedom from all curses on the cross through the atonement of His blood, why is the ground still cursed? (Gen. 3:17, Rev. 22:1-3.) Because there is a time lapse between God's *promise* and its fulfillment. God's promises of blessings *or* curses (judgment) rarely occur immediately, in our time frame.

The Promised Land belonged to Israel when Joseph was first taken to Egypt to be sold as a slave as much as it did four hundred years later when Moses led Israel out of bondage. The land belonged to them no less when they fled across the Red Sea in front of Pharoah's army than it did forty years later when their children possessed the land. But Israel had a part to play in the possessing of what was already theirs—they had to *take* it.

All born again believers have freedom from the penalty of the law—separation from God—and from the consequences of transgressions, ancestral and their own. But they *have to receive that freedom in faith.* Bondages of evil spirits or the "sludge" of the old nature keep many people from receiving freedom just as the bondages of fear, pride, and rebellion kept a generation of Israelites from receiving the Promised Land. They were delivered from bondage to Egypt, but remained in bondage to Satan.

Many believers received freedom from the penalty of "death" (eternal separation from God), but have not received

The Curse Causeless Shall Not Come

freedom in their everyday lives. They have been resurrected but not loosed and cleansed. They have been taken out of "Egypt" to the Promised Land, but their souls and bodies are still in bondage to Satan and to the world (Sodom, meaning violence and all sins of the appetite, and Babylon, world economy, cultures and lifestyle). They need to be loosed and cleansed. Eddie Traut of South Africa told me something very important:

"Christians walk through life and pick up spiritual dirt but never think of taking a spiritual bath, when they are very meticulous about taking a natural bath to wash off the dirt of an everyday walk in the earth."

The "blessings and cursings" that affect most people today were spoken by God long *after* the curse of death fell on mankind through Adam and Eve. They stem from the covenant between God and Abraham. Why do they affect believers today as well as the Israelites, and later, the Jews? Because, the Holy Spirit wrote through the apostle Paul, *we are the children of Abraham* as truly through Jesus, the true or real Seed of Promise, as the Israelites were through Isaac, the type or symbolic Seed of Promise.

> **For ye are all the children of God by faith in Christ Jesus.**
>
> **For as many of you as have been baptized into Christ have put on Christ.**
>
> **There is neither Jew nor Greek, there is neither bond nor free, there is neither male nor female: for ye are all one in Christ Jesus.**
>
> **And if ye be Christ's, *then are ye Abraham's seed*, and heirs according to the promise.**
>
> **Galatians 3:26-29**

> **Now we, brethren, as Isaac was, are the children of promise.**
>
> **Galatians 4:28**

The "blessings and cursings" of the Old Testament are *covenant promises* to the seed of Abraham, which Paul said Christians are. (Gal. 3:29.) Blessings and cursings are the consequences of maintaining the conditions of the covenant—which applies now to all believers—or of breaking them. Why? Because God never changes, and the provisions are still in effect through a better covenant made by the Son of God and the Seed of Abraham—Jesus.

All of Paul's writings about being no longer under the law were aimed at those Jewish Christians who attempted to make the religious statutes (sacrifices, unclean meats, rituals of ceremonial washings, and so forth) a prerequisite for being born again. He was at great pains to say the Promise to Abraham overrides the Law (civil and religious statutes) given to Moses hundreds of years later. The *blessings and curses* still in effect for believers today stem from the Promise. God had not spelled them out until Mount Sinai, but all of them are specific results of *hearing and obeying* Him or *not* hearing and obeying Him—the "clauses" of the Abrahamic covenant.

> **For I know him, that he will command his *children* and his *household* after him, and they shall keep the way of the Lord** (hear and obey), **to do justice and judgment; that the Lord may bring upon Abraham** (and his seed, or household) **that which he** (God) **hath spoken of him.**
> **Genesis 18:19**

In Isaiah, the Lord again spelled out what will happen to those who break the *everlasting covenant*—the old covenant fulfilled in the new, which is even a better covenant (Isa. 24:5):

> **Therefore hath the *curse* devoured the earth, and they that dwell therein are desolate: therefore the inhabitants of the earth are burned, and few men left.**
> **Isaiah 24:6**

The context of the verse is the end times. If the freedom from God's curses had been *accomplished* and not just *provided for*—or purchased—by Jesus, famine, plagues, drought, and the sword would not still be among believers as well as sinners. What is true in general must be true specifically. Freedom from covenant curses, old or new, must be received individually.

In the new covenant, Jesus said, the Law and the prophets (in the sense of God's principles which we are required to obey) were summed up in **love the Lord thy God with all your heart** and **love your neighbor as yourself** (Matt. 22:37-39). The religious laws, or statutes, were fulfilled in Jesus, which we commemorate in the sacrament of Communion. The civil laws of Israel and Judah are replaced by the civil laws of our own country—which we are to obey (Rom. 13:1-3) as long as those laws do not violate God's higher laws and His worship.

Many Christians today are inconsistent in their theological beliefs, or their interpretation of God's Word. They claim the blessings of the Abrahamic covenant, but want to do away with the curses! Believers need to know it is necessary to break curses in order to enjoy blessings. One must tithe and give to the poor (obedience to God in finances, or making Jesus Lord of your money) in order to break the curse of poverty and enjoy the blessings of prosperity in this life. (Mal. 3:8-10, Prov. 28:27.) Tithing as works or religious ritual or duty—for outward appearances—will not break the curse. God looks at the inward man and at motives. Blessings come from giving one's tithe cheerfully (2 Cor. 9:7), from giving obediently as unto the Lord.

Ancestral Curses, or Consequences of Generational Sin

Many people can see the logic of curses, or consequences, stemming from their own actions of commission or omission. But they have a problem with believing specific problems in their lives might be the result of a curse on them from an ancestor's transgression. Their "proof" usually is Ezekiel 18:1-4, which is considered to be God's revocation of a sentence He had passed on the Israelites. Ezekiel wrote:

> The word of the Lord came unto me again, saying,
>
> What mean ye, that ye use this proverb concerning the land of Israel, saying, The fathers have eaten sour grapes, and the children's teeth are set on edge?
>
> As I live, saith the Lord God, ye shall not have occasion any more to use this proverb in Israel.
>
> Behold, all souls are mine; as the soul of the father, so also the soul of the son is mine: the soul that sinneth, it shall die.

Many people use this to prove that God changed His mind about the earlier "curse" and rescinded it. They say He was stressing individual responsibility for one's own blessings and cursings. However, if you go by systematic theology in interpreting the Bible and use the "Law of First Reference,"[2] you will find those words first in Jeremiah 31:29, 30 in a prophecy. This word from God apparently was about complete accomplishing of provisions of the new covenant in the Millennium, because the passage ends with this verse:

> And the whole valley of the dead bodies, and of the ashes, and all the fields unto the brook of Kidron, unto the corner of the horse gate toward the east, shall be holy unto the Lord; it shall not be plucked up, nor thrown down any more for ever.
>
> Jeremiah 31:40

The new covenant is in effect, and the *law* mentioned in Jeremiah 31:33 and Hebrews 8:10 has been written in our spirits, but the complete fulfillment of all that God promised

The Curse Causeless Shall Not Come

has not yet arrived. Complete exoneration from the sins of the fathers has been *provided*, but each person must yet *receive* that pardon to have any ancestral curses become inoperative in his life—although freedom from that curse was provided on the cross. After the Second Coming, when sanctification is complete past, present, and future, there will be no more curse of any kind: The **whole valley of the dead** (the entire spirits, souls, and bodies of believers) **shall be holy unto the Lord.** They will **not be plucked up, nor thrown down any more for ever.** (We are aware that this verse has a literal meaning about the city of Jerusalem as well as a spiritual meaning.)

The consequences or results of generational sin come on us in three ways:[3]

1. Heredity—physical, personality, and behavior.

2. Environment—copying what parents and grandparents did.

3. Law of sowing and reaping—harvests are not always immediate. One reason for ancestral transgressions affecting us is that we were "in their loins" when they committed the sins. (Precedent: Heb. 7:10.) God's law was designed to perpetuate blessings, but its opposite reaction came into operation when darkness covered the world and its people after Adam and Eve. That darkness has not yet been removed in manifestation, although it has in reality—positionally, not experientially. (Read the book of Revelation.)

Those who say this is "not fair" need to be reminded that we reap blessings from our ancestors (inventions, ways of life, good health as well as bad). Every law has two sides: freedom and penalty, blessings and curses, even in this world. It is not possible to reap the good from good seeds without reaping the bad from bad seeds.

The Lord has made it very clear to Gloria and to me—from Scripture and from the results we see in believers' lives when curses have been broken—that His judgments for *not hearing and obeying* are still in effect. (In the Appendix is a list of some of the specific judgments or curses for disobedience found in the Bible.)

In addition, there are curses pronounced by other people with which many have to deal. The Old Testament contains several examples of men of God pronouncing curses that were as binding as those of God Himself. Joshua set a curse on any man who rebuilt Jericho after the Israelites took the city by marching around it seven times, then burned it up. The curse was fulfilled in 1 Kings 16:34.

Indications That Point to the Presence of a Curse

Evangelist Derek Prince in *From Curse to Blessing*[4] lists seven indications he has found as common denominators that show up evidencing the presence of a curse. They are:

1. Mental and/or emotional breakdowns.

2. Repeated or chronic sicknesses, especially if they are hereditary or have no medical diagnoses.

3. Repeated miscarriages or female problems.

4. Breakdown of marriages and family alienation.

5. Financial problems when the income appears to be sufficient. (We would add, "repeated and unexplainable attacks or drains on finances.")

6. Someone or a family who is accident prone.

7. A history of suicides or unnatural deaths.

If all of these, and other things, keep showing up in a family, it is more than likely that a generational curse is operating.

End Notes

1. *Oxford American Dictionary*, p. 156.
2. The *Law of the First Reference* is a term theologians use that means the true meaning of a passage of Scripture should be interpreted by its meaning the first time it occurs in the Bible.
3. Sandford, *Healing the Wounded Spirit*, pp. 369-391.
4. Derek Prince. *From Curse to Blessing* (A transcription of the radio program, *Today With Derek Prince*, Weekly Series #138 & #139.) Derek Prince Ministries, P. O. Box 300, Fort Lauderdale, Florida 33302), p. 19.

5
How Do We Give Place to the Devil?

Demons cannot harass believers without a "legal" right. And what "curses" really mean is that certain areas of a person's life are not covered by the protection of God. If those are not under God's rule, or Kingdom, you fall under the devil's rule. The influence or oppression by demons in a Christian's life is a sure indication of a curse in operation.

One of the easiest examples is *fear*. The Bible says God does not give us a spirit of fear. (2 Tim. 1:7.) Therefore, in any area where you have fear, you are not "hearing and obeying" God. You are then under the judgment—curse or consequence—and liable to any harassment of demons that enter through fear. They usually bring other spirits along, such as various sicknesses, mental and emotional as well as physical. But all of those things are results of a curse that became valid in your life through an area over which Jesus is not Lord. Sins of the flesh or of the soul (mind, will, or emotions) bring the curse for not "hearing and obeying."

Proverbs 26:2 (AMP) says:

> As the sparrow in her wandering, as the swallow in her flying, so the causeless curse shall not alight.

Whether ancestral, personal, or corporate (as a local church, the Body entirely, or one's city, state, or nation), all curses boil down to the two root causes of not hearing or not obeying God.

Demons Must Have Open Doors to Attack

The forces of Satan cannot enter a believer's soul or body without an open door. Demons have control in the lives of believers who are ignorant of spiritual warfare, and doctrines against deliverance keep believers in ignorance—which the devil loves.

This is why Paul wrote, **Neither give place to the devil** (Eph. 4:27), and James wrote, **Submit yourselves therefore to God's word then resist the devil, and he will flee from you** (James 4:7). Paraphrase.

In addition to heredity (ancestral curses, physical conditions and disabilities, and so forth), open doors include negative emotions, occult involvement, unrepented sin, and negative words, prayers, and confession. The last three are curses pronounced on oneself. (Followers of the Word-Faith movement recognize these things but call them "negative confessions" and do not recognize that a curse by any other name is still a curse!)

Curses Pronounced on Oneself and One's Descendants

The ultimate consequence of any curse, unless otherwise specified, is destruction of whatever area is involved. One example of a curse pronounced on oneself is Rebecca.

> And Jacob said to Rebekah his mother . . . My father peradventure will feel me, and I shall seem to him as a de-

How Do We Give Place to the Devil?

> ceiver; and I shall bring a curse upon me, and not a blessing.
> And his mother said unto him, Upon me be thy curse, my son: only obey my voice, and go fetch me them.
> Genesis 27:11a-13.

She died before ever seeing Jacob again. Another example is:

> **Then answered all the people, and said, His blood be on us, and on our children.**
> **Matthew 27:25**

The curse, or consequence, of shedding innocent blood was to be ruled and oppressed by those who hate you (Ps. 106:38-42) and an early death. In Matthew 27:4, the acceptance of responsibility for the crucifixion of Jesus ("let the curse be on us and our children") along with non-recognition of the Messiah is the root cause of the problems of the Jews over the past two thousand years. Shedding innocent blood also is listed as one of the seven things that are an abomination to God. (Prov. 6:17.)

Many believers speak curses over themselves more often than they realize: "Nothing ever turns out right for me," "I know I'll catch this virus going around," "I never have enough money." There are several admonitions in Proverbs about this:

> **Thou art snared with the words of thy mouth, thou art taken with the words of thy mouth** (6:2).
> **There is that speaketh like the piercings of a sword: but the tongue of the wise is health** (12:18).
> **A wholesome tongue is a tree of life: but perverseness therein is a breach in the spirit** (15:4).
> **Death and life are in the power of the tongue: and they that love it shall eat the fruit thereof** (18:21).

Loose Them and Let Them Go

James wrote in the New Testament about the power of the tongue for blessings *and* cursings. (James 3:1-10.)

Curses Pronounced by Others

Curses can be pronounced on a believer through witchcraft or hexes, through words spoken by those in authority over you (although they do not realize those words constitute curses), and through words spoken by someone in whom you believe. Witchcraft and hexes will be covered in the next chapter, but the classic Biblical example of a curse spoken over someone by an authority figure is that of Rachel. When Jacob fled the territory of his father-in-law, Laban, with his wives, children, and belongings, Rachel also took along the gods (images) that belonged to her father's house. Her motive apparently was greed, because whoever possessed the household gods in that culture was the legal inheritor. But she did this without the knowledge of Jacob. So when Laban followed them, as much for the gods as to tell his daughters and grandchildren farewell, Jacob said (not knowing he was cursing the wife whom he loved):

With whomsoever thou findest thy gods, let him not live.
Genesis 31:32

Jacob had authority over his wife, and the sequel which happened a short time later is found in Genesis 35:19.

And Rachel died (in childbirth), and was buried in the way to Ephrath, which is Bethlehem.

David was king of Israel and had authority over all of the people and double authority as commander-in-chief over all the officers of his army. He knowingly pronounced a curse on

How Do We Give Place to the Devil?

Joab, all of his father's house, and his descendants for murdering Abner who was under a "flag of truce." Actually, what David did was transfer the curse from himself and his kingdom onto the guilty person and his relatives. David pronounced a fearful curse on Joab's relatives.

> **Let it rest on the head of Joab, and on all his father's house; and let there not fail from the house of Joab one that hath an issue, or that is a leper, or that leaneth on a staff, or that falleth on the sword, or that lacketh bread.**
> **2 Samuel 3:29**

That curse included leprosy, being handicapped, dying in war, and poverty. Quite a curse! It makes you wonder where the descendants of Joab are scattered today!

In reality, anything you speak over your children that is derogatory, that is negative or harmful, may result in a curse. If you call them stupid or clumsy or "no good," you are giving the devil free reign to enter and make that happen. Many people who come to us have to be freed from these kinds of curses.

In a Kenneth Copeland meeting in Tulsa, Oklahoma, during the fall of 1987, an example of curses by others was graphically told. A young lady who came forward to testify of healing told a story of accident after accident that had caused her serious injuries since the age of 10. Several times, she had received miraculous healings not only through her own faith but through the laying on of hands.

As she was speaking, the Lord showed Copeland and evangelist Jerry Savelle that she had been under a curse, and He instructed them to break it, which they did.

Then Wayne Cochran (famous for his blues record, *C. C. Rider* and now a nationally known evangelist) came forward and said the Lord showed him a neighbor woman had pronounced a curse over the girl unknowingly when she was 10 years old. Apparently, she had called her clumsy or said something that gave demons a legal right to cause the girl to be injured time after time. (The world calls that "accident prone.") He also said God was going to allow this young lady to remember who that person was and to go back home and lead her to the Lord. But they warned the girl not to ever call herself "accident prone" or to allow anyone else to do so. The devil would like to reactivate that curse.

One of our relatives who did not believe Christians could have demons constantly had problems in her life—accidents, sicknesses, not being able to keep a job, and so forth. Finally, she allowed Jimmy to pray with her, and he bound a control spirit from operating in her life. Then he asked her, a Christian, if she would like to see whether she had demons affecting her or not. When she agreed, he began taking authority over and casting out evil spirits of destruction, death, and infirmity *after he prayed the Prayer of Protection.* (See Appendix.) We broke all the curses applicable in her life from generational inheritances (occult practices in her American Indian bloodline) and from things in her own life. Since that day, her life has changed. She obtained the job she desired and has been able to keep it. She has had no more accidents and is happily married.

Some of the worst afflictions believers have today stem from ancestral occult practices or from those committed by believers themselves. People can open the door to occult spirits through many seemingly harmless things that permeate today's culture.

6
Detestable Things

God made it very clear that coming into contact with things known to be of Satan brings a curse on you, on your children, your grandchildren, and your great-grandchildren.

> . . . **For I the Lord thy God am a jealous God, visiting the iniquity of the fathers upon the children unto the third and fourth generation of them that hate me.**
> **Deuteronomy 5:9,10**

God obviously considers those who traffic in the devil's realm as **those who hate me.** The Bible calls the supernatural works of the devil detestable things and says those who do them are detestable to the Lord. *The King James Version* uses *abomination*, but the implication is the same: God hates them.

> **Anyone who does these things is** *detestable* **to the Lord, and because of** *the detestable practices* **the Lord your God will drive out those nations before you.**
> **Deuteronomy 18:12 NIV**

"These things," as found in Deuteronomy 18:10 and 11, are:

1. *Human sacrifices* to Satan (causing one's son or daughter to pass through the fire). Cannibalism is an outgrowth of this. Also, abortion amounts to a sacrifice to Satan.
2. *Divination*—attempting to look into the future, a counterfeit of one aspect of the ministry of the gift of prophecy. This includes fortunetellers, tea-leaf readers, and palm or card readers. A diviner also was known as a "soothsayer," the pagan counterpart of a prophet who was a seer.
3. *Observing of times*—The aspect of astrology that predicts the future is divination, also called stargazing.
4. *Enchanters*—using incantations to "call up" a demon to assist in some purpose. Magicians (not those who use sleight of hand and eye to entertain, but those who use the power of Satan to achieve "magic" accomplishments) are also called "enchanters."
5. *Witchcraft*—bewitching or putting curses and hexes on people through "magic" rituals or incantations; used in modern times as synonymous with "charmer." Unwittingly practiced by many Christians who speak words against someone else—gossip, lying, manipulating, and false prophecies.
6. *Charmers*—We believe this refers to hypnotists; in Old Testament days, this was a reference to the technique of "snake charming" which could be extended to humans as hypnotism.
7. *Consulting with familiar spirits*—"spiritism" or spiritualism, allegedly calling up a dead person. People operating in this area are sometimes called mediums.
8. *Wizardry*—the male form of witchcraft, sometimes known as warlocks.
9. *Necromancy*—using objects to consult with the dead in order to gain knowledge of the future, seances or "table-tapping," ouija boards.

Detestable Things

10. *Sorcery*—a general term for all satanic supernatural trafficing. The Greek word for sorcery, *pharmakeia*, is also the word from which our drug or medicine-related words, such as pharmacy, are derived. Those operating in sorcery many times used herbs in their spells. The first meaning of the Greek word is "medicine, drugs, spells; then poisoning; then sorcery."[1] This connection is why drug addicts open the door to affliction by occult spirits. All these things give demons legal access to your mind, as drug and alcohol addiction do. Jesus called the devil's ways *sorcery:*

> . . . for by thy sorceries were all nations deceived.
> **Revelation 18:23**

Some people operating in hypnotism, witchcraft, fortune telling or astrology may not know they are using satanic powers, but the consequences will be the same as if they did know. (The law of gravity goes into effect whether a child knows what will happen if he jumps off a building or not.) Principles of the universe are unchangeable, which is why so much evil resulted from man's fall in the Garden. God will forgive you for breaking His laws, but He will not change the laws. They are inherent in His character, and His entire universe is built on them as expressed in His Word. A sorcerer adds wilfull *intent* to his breaking of God's laws. He *knows* he is using supernatural powers to manipulate nature or cause things to happen to certain people.

Many witches' covens[2]—especially in the past twenty or twenty-five years—have used sorcery to attack ministries and churches. Satanic cults pray for Christians to die, to fall into adultery (especially ministries), and to experience financial problems. They even pray with chants and incantations for television and sound equipment to fail.

God is not only against those who knowingly practice the *detestable things,* but He is just as adamant about those who only participate in them. Doing these things or allowing them to be done to or for you, even in fun, amounts to idolatry for any person and to spiritual adultery against God if you are already a believer.

In Leviticus, God made it clear how serious these things are:

> **I will set my face against the person who turns to mediums and to spiritists, to prostitute himself by following them, and I will cut him off from his people.**
> **Leviticus 20:6 NIV**

Other forms of occultism are perhaps better known today than those listed in the Old Testament. Most of them can be found operating in groups or individuals in the New Age movement. Few Americans have not been exposed to some of these things. I believe that in the 1960s demons that previously had been operating solely in "heathen" countries began to move into Western, "free" nations.

Modern Forms of Occult Trafficking

Names of other occult practices more familiar in our society include:

1. *Clairvoyance*—knowing or seeing things about people supernatually, the satanic counterpart of the Holy Spirit's gifts of the words of wisdom and knowledge. Also known as "second sight" or "use of the third eye" (supposedly in the center of the forehead.)
Clairaudience—hearing things about someone else supernaturally, falls into the same category.
Clairsentience— the sensing of an unseen presence or thought, the counterfeit of intuitive hunches from the Holy Spirit through a believer's spirit called a "witness" or a "knowing."

2. The *I Ching* or *pendulum* or *dowsing* (water witching)—forms of divination.

Detestable Things 49

3. *Cartomancy*—divination through the laying of cards, tarot or ordinary playing cards.

4. *Ventriloquism*—used in pagan religious rites, involves deception. Many people think this can be learned, but what really happens is that by attempting to "learn" the techniques, they open themselves up to familiar spirits. One secular ventriloquist who used to appear on a well-known country variety show manifested this "ability" before he could talk. His family and baby sitters at first were upset by hearing him crying in other rooms or across the room from his crib until they saw he was "throwing his voice." As he grew up, he was encouraged in developing his "talent."

Ventriloquists in ancient times were sometimes called "belly" prophets.

> **And if they should say unto you, Seek those who have a divining spirit, and them that speak out of the earth** (mediums or spiritists), **them that speak vain words, who speak out of their belly** (ventriloquists): **should not a nation diligently seek to their God? why do they seek to the dead concerning the living?**
>
> Isaiah 8:19[3]

Many believers today operate in "Christian ventriloquism," but their lives are usually afflicted with sicknesses, accidents, divorce, financial problems in spite of tithing and giving—in other words, all of the things that are involved in a curse that follows participation in occult arts. Some deliverance ministers even feel that puppets and dolls or stuffed animals should be banned. We believe these things *can* be focal points from which demons may gain legal entrance into otherwise "clean" families. However, we do not believe that this is true without exception. The best thing to do is pray and seek the guidance of the Holy Spirit.

5. *Astral travel*—projection of one's spirit out of the body by the help of demons (spirit guides). This is practiced by me-

diums, yoga devotees, and inadvertently sometimes, by drug users. This can result in demon possession, mental illness (when the mind cannot accept what it sees in the Second Heaven or becomes oppressed by demons), or death (if the spirit is prevented from getting back to the body). This is Satan's counterfeit of believers' experiences such as the apostle Paul's visit to the Third Heaven (2 Cor. 12:2) under the protection of God. The difference is that God initiates believers' visits to heaven or hell. We cannot *decide* to visit either.

6. *Acupuncture* in any of its forms—Rooted in ancient Chinese religious (pagan) practices.

7. *Mind-oriented operations*—meditation, mind control, expanded consciousness, self-hypnosis, or mental "games." These include such things as Transcendental Meditation (idolatry), EST, yoga, dungeons and dragons and its spin-offs, also many video games. All of these involve sharing one's mind with a familiar spirit.

8. *Voodoo-type arts, "black magic," or "white" witchcraft*—use of supernatural help to manipulate another person's life for "good" or "bad" purposes against their will and usually without their being aware of the manipulation.

Many people came into the Charismatic move untaught in the Scriptures or straight from false religions without getting deliverance. A few of them have fallen into *"Charismatic witchcraft."* A number of "Charismatic witches" rule over little groups across the country through "prophecies" and "revelations."

For example, praying for someone's business to fail so he will "develop more faith in God" is nothing but witchcraft. "Claiming" someone else's house or car is not faith but covetousness and witchcraft—unless God first tells you it is yours, in which case, He already has plans for the other people's good. Otherwise, such praying is not only presumption but witchcraft. Those people who pulled the movement of

Detestable Things

discipleship off balance and destroyed its credibility a few years ago were operating in soul power, not authority (covering), and many fell into witchcraft.

Parents who use mind control techniques or even physical abuse to manipulate their children are operating in witchcraft. Such parents need deliverance and cleansing, and the children need deliverance, inner healing, and cleansing through forgiveness.

Prayer can be another form of religious witchcraft when people of satanic-ruled or infiltrated religions "pray" for others who have "left the faith" or whom they are "claiming." Those prayers, usually prayed on holy or feast days, constitute incantations that authorize demons to afflict those prayed for. The results are curses. These are counterfeits of claiming a family's salvation. (James 3:8–11.)

9. *Psychometry*—modern variation of necromancy in which objects are used not only to "read" things about a dead person but to find out things about a living person. Sometimes objects such as a shirt or handkerchief are used in "psychic healings," a counterpart of the healing cloths used by the Church.

10. *Psychiatry*—secular counseling in the disciplines of many atheistic founders (Freud, Jung, Skinner, and so forth), the world's counterfeit of Bible truths on sanctification. There may be truths in psychiatry, but the source is not God. Many times, psychiatrists operate in a false spirit of discernment and/or witchcraft, which is why so many fall into sexual sins with their clients.

11. *Extrasensory powers or psychic phenomena*—covers many aspects of satanic supernatural manifestations, including psychometry, telepathy (mind reading), apports (demon-manifested objects, many times feathers or paper that later disintegrates), telekinesis or psychokinesis (moving objects even through closed doors or bending objects allegedly by

mind control). Flying saucers or little green men sightings fall under this category. This involves the ability to influence or change the present or future.

12. *Extrasensory perception* (ESP)—being able to perceive supernatural things with the natural mind, a counterfeit of discernment of spirits and the prophetic ministries of the Holy Spirit. Also defined as the ability to supernaturally *know* the past, present, and future.

13. *Parapsychology*—the "scientific" research into extrasensory perception. Many large universities and colleges not only offer courses in parapsychology but fund "chairs" (professorships) in this field now. Several special laboratories for ESP investigations have been established, such as the Rhine Institute at Duke University in North Carolina. They are modern counterparts of witches' schools of the Middle Ages and temple schools of pagan religions (such as the temple to Diana of Ephesus mentioned in Acts 19:35). However, the pagan "schools" mixed sexual license and perversion with their training, teaching, and investigations of the occult, and modern parapsychology schools do not.

14. *Spirit writing*—a familiar spirit takes control of a person's arm and "writes" for them. The handwriting is different than the person's own. This is the same mediumistic operation as *speaking in a trance* because many times the person writes in a trance—a counterfeit of the Holy Spirit's anointing for writing or speaking, in which case the believer is in his or her right mind and not being "controlled" but *inspired*. The "person" speaking in a trance is the demon, and the voice is different usually from that of the host.

15. *Levitation*—the alleged ability to lift oneself (or objects) off the ground or floor and stay suspended in the air for certain lengths of time. Yoga includes this in its teachings, as do several other Eastern philosophies and religions. In reality, the person or object is being lifted or moved by a demon. *Poltergeist* phenomena fall under this heading. They occur of-

Detestable Things

ten when a demon is able to utilize the sexual energy of a young person in puberty. The movie and book, *Amityville Horror,* was a very exaggerated, "hokey" version of true accounts of this kind of activity, plus other demonic manifestations. Other movies depicting *poltergeist* phenomena include *Close Encounters* and *Poltergeist,* also *Gremlins.*

16. *Martial "arts"* — the ability to do superhuman feats with the body. "Christian" karate (or similar sports) is a contradiction in terms. The person may be a Christian, but the power to do these things is not from God and cannot be done by the human body alone, no matter how much exercise and practise are involved. All *martial arts* can be traced to ancient Oriental religions and remain religions, not physical disciplines. The underlying principle is mind-body coordination through a combination of exercises and meditations.

17. *Metaphysical phenomena* — the sighting of apparitions and ghosts, which are in reality demon spirits. A "haunted" place or house is one which has a demon assigned or attached to it.

18. *Psychic healing*—"surgery" and other medical practices done through the aid of spirit guides, a counterfeit of the Holy Spirit's ministry of healing through the laying on of hands.

19. *Sensitivity training*—many industrial companies are using this, but not to the extent it is being employed in Japan's business community! Some of the mind-oriented programs are included in this. However, in any form, it moves from the good objective of being sensitive to others' feelings to brain washing. Many cults use forms of this. Participants must go through "de-programming" *and* deliverance. Otherwise, they remain "zombies."

20. *Precognition*—knowing events (usually deaths, accidents, and so forth) before they happen, another counterfeit of the Holy Spirit's prophetic flashes (mini-visions), words that prepare Christians for oncoming events or warn them to

pray. The devil's precognition is easy to distinguish: it always brings fear, even horror, and the feeling of powerlessness. The Holy Spirit's warnings are always cushioned in peace. (James 3:17.) There are never any negative or carnal emotions connected with His messages.

21. *Observance of omens*—this involves putting faith in any superstition or sign, such as "an owl hooting means a death in the family," and so forth.

22. *Astrology*—the occult "art" that is more popular today than any of the others and than it has been for hundreds of years. In fact, this seemingly harmless activity is often the "door" to many other occult practices. Astrology has several forms today: popular newspaper and magazine columns; in-depth charts and counseling; geographical astrology which uses your birth chart to figure out the best latitude and longitude for you to live; charts based on moon *or* sun signs; and "seasonal" prognostications, such as *Earth, Air, Fire, and Water,* or winter, summer, fall, and spring quarters.

This last form has crept into the Church under the guise of "color-draping" or "color-coding." It seems harmless and fashion effective, but it involves calling a person by the names of the seasons: "You are a winter person or a fall person," and so forth. In open astrological terms, the same program is used but begins by finding the birthday in order to find the color. The devil loves to use the spectacular, especially color, to pull people under his authority. Satanic visions often use color to make people think they are from God: "That was so real, it had to be God." What they mean is that the vision or apparition or supernatural event was so close to all the hokey effects of recent movies that it had to be supernatural, therefore it had to be God. Satan specializes in blue-light apparitions and effects.

In the next chapter, we will discuss how to discern the spirits or how to judge supernatural happenings.

Detestable Things

Unclean Objects

Many Christians today who have never participated in even one instance of palm reading or other occult practice have come under the influence of occult demons through bringing *unclean objects* into their homes. Again, it should be pointed out that ignorance or innocence is no protection when violating these laws of God. Sometimes the consequences will not be quite as bad in these cases because blessings in other areas offset some of the curse, or because the person's faith in God's protection overrides the curse. Nevertheless, keeping cursed things in one's home is a dangerous procedure.

> **Neither shalt thou bring an abomination into thine house, lest thou be an accursed thing like it: but thou shalt utterly detest it, and thou shalt utterly abhor it; for it is a cursed thing.**
> **Deuteronomy 7:26**

Accursed things include statuettes or objets d'art that represent idols or false gods, unclean animals (owls, bats, frogs, spiders, snakes, flies, and so forth); jewelry or amulets that depict these things; charms, such as four-leaf clovers or rabbit's feet or horseshoes, as well as zodiac symbols and the Egyptian ankh; and even toys when they depict the occult characters on today's "cartoon" shows or science fiction characters.[4] Turquoise jewelry in American Indian witchcraft designs is very much sought after today. The Kachina dolls of the Southwest are nothing but idols of Hopi Indian demon-gods. Even having glassware in the house with Kachinas on it, or paintings, means you have an *accursed thing* in your house.

Incense also is an abomination because it has been used from time immemorial in the rituals of false religions and because, most of the time even today, it is made in countries under demon control and by people who place curses on it during its manufacture.

Anything advertised as "good luck" or "healing" articles, such as copper jewelry, and things made of lapis lazuli (the "white stone" symbol of alchemy, the occult art of transmuting base things into precious things, such as iron into gold). In addition, many times, these items are being made and/or sold by witches' covens, New Age companies, or astrology-based firms, which may add "spells."

Unclean animals are those associated in the Bible with witchcraft or idol worship. Anything used in ancient Egypt or Babylon usually is *accursed*. All of the plagues that were sent on the Egyptians through Moses involved animals or insects worshipped as gods or sacred to the demon-gods. Possibly, these animals are easier for demons to possess[5], although instances of cats and dogs being possessed are well-known. Egypt had a cat goddess and a dog-faced god.

Sexual problems usually compound those stemming from occult involvement. Demons that operate in occult practices also seem to bring in sexual addiction, perversion, and related problems such as pornography.

End Notes

1. *Vine's Expository Dictionary,* Vol. 4, p. 52.
2. A "witches' coven" is a satanic counterpart to Jesus and the twelve disciples. Thirteen people band together to partake in satanic rituals, send out curses, or in other occultic practices.
3. Sir Lancelot C.L. Brenton, *The Septuagint With Apocrypha:* Greek and English (Michigan: Grand Rapids, Zondervan Publishing House, 1983. Originally published, 1851, by Samuel Bagster & Sons, London, England.
4. Phil Phillips, *Turmoil in the Toy Box* (Pennsylvania: Lancaster. Starburst Publishers, P. O. Box 4123, 1986).
5. Worley, "Annihilating the Hosts of Hell," *The Battle Royal: Book II,* p. 106.

7
How to Tell the True From the False

There are several ways to measure or test the true against the false. One standard against which supernatural events can be measured is the character of God as revealed in the Bible and in Jesus.

I. *The character and ways of God:*
   A. *He never does anything capriciously, to show off and "prove" He is God, or without a purpose.*

      Jesus walked on the water for a very pragmatic reason: to get to the other side of the lake. He would have passed the disciples if they had not happened to see Him. (Mark 6:48.) He multiplied loaves and fishes for a very practical reason: to feed the hungry, not to prove He was God. He rebuked some of those following for making His ability to meet their physical needs the basis for belief. (John 6:26.)

      Angels appeared to bring messages or to carry out God's instructions or to minister to prophets and saints—not to usurp the Holy Spirit's role as Counselor and Teacher or to start new religions (such as Islam, Bahai, and Mormonism). Philip was supernaturally transported by the Spirit of the Lord (Acts 8:39,40) because God wanted him in another place (Azotus) to preach—not to cause Philip to become puffed up or even to keep him from having to walk there.

God may do things in the last days of "the last days" (which began with the resurrection of Jesus) that have never been seen before and whose exact counterpart may not be in the Bible. However, *in principle they will be the same.* God's supernatural events are reasonable and occur in an atmosphere of peace, not one of excitement. The people who were fed with the loaves and fishes sat quietly and in order, and the whole event seemed "natural" at the time. Nor does God encourage speculation beyond what we are told. (Col. 4:6.)

B. *God does not do things in secret* (Isa. 48:16, Dan. 2:22,). In Amos 3:7, God made this very plain.

Surely the Sovereign Lord does nothing without revealing his plan to his servants the prophets. NIV

One sure sign of satanic influence is a philosophy, an organization, or a teaching with secret rites or beliefs, or with memberships secret initiations. These are counterfeits of the Body of Christ, groups through which desires to belong to a "family" can be falsely satisfied—a pacifier instead of real milk.

C. *God does not do anything for show.*

For example, those who have "signs" (bleeding) in the palms of their hands, the alleged "stigmata" of Jesus, are under the operation of a familiar spirit.

Why? Because there is no Biblical basis for it, in kind or in character, and it serves no purpose but to single them out as different or special, to draw attention to the person and not Jesus. The history of such things goes back to the worship of saints (idolatry) and usually was associated with women who abused their bodies through flagellation or extreme asceticism.

The "signs and wonders" that are to follow the preaching of the Gospel *are for the purpose of ministry* to believers or to those about to become believers— not for God to "show off." These "signs and wonders" are practical ministry: physical healings, creative miracles, and casting out of demons, not spectacular supernatural occurences. Occult participation always "puffs up" the person (and the demon behind him). The man named Simon whom Philip ran across in Samaria is a good example:

But there was a certain man, called Simon, which beforetime in the same city used sorcery, and bewitched the people of Samaria, *giving out that himself was some great one:*

To whom they all gave heed, from the least to the greatest, saying, This man is the great power of God.

And to him they had regard, *because that of long time he had bewitched them with sorceries.*
Acts 8:9-11

How many Christians have followed "supernatural signs" and fallen to the wiles of the devil? How many have ended up ministering in a mixture of their calling from God *and* occult signs and wonders?

One Charismatic evangelist who somehow fell into this ended up with a ministry that utilized hypnotism. The people who were "slain in the Spirit" fell forward, not backward as is customary, which created awkward moments for those ushers catching the women being ministered to. Some people on whom he laid hands writhed in the floor like snakes. He called it "God's chiropractic," but it was demonic.

II. A second standard by which to measure is *whether the Biblical Jesus is upheld*.

True ministry always will uphold the preeminence and lordship of Jesus *as He is revealed in the Bible*. If Jesus is the center of the teaching—and if it maintains the integrity of His ways and character from the Word—then the teaching must have truth. If the teaching centers on Jesus but maintains that He condemns Christians, or wants them to break spiritual or natural laws, or teaches that salvation is earned *or kept* through works, that doctrine holds up "another Jesus" (1 Cor. 8:6) than the One in the Bible.

Scriptures that uphold this principle are found in Philippians 2:1-11; 1 Corinthians 12; Ephesians 1:18-23, 2:20, 3:14,15, 4:15, 5:23, 6:10; and Colossians 1:12-20, 2:6-10,18,19.

III. *Other standards:* Christians can judge supernatural things by a witness from the Holy Spirit, by patterns or examples in the Word, by the fruits of the phenomena (peace or negative things), by the purposes of the happening (to glorify Jesus or to glorify man), and by the fruit of the person through whom they operate.

A prophet may preach entirely Biblical doctrines, yet the fruit of his ministry be negative things. The man mentioned above preached sermons above reproach, but his meetings were followed by a trail of suicides, physical problems, and host ministers whose minds became afflicted by spirits of forgetfulness and confusion. In the last days, we are told there will be false doctrines

How to Tell the True From the False

and false prophets—not necessarily manifesting in the same person. Everything should be judged by the Spirit (Holy Spirit) and truth (the Bible).

But the wisdom that is from above is first pure, then peaceable, gentle, and easy to be entreated, full of mercy and good fruits, without partiality, and without hypocrisy.

James 3:17

The ministry of the gift of tongues if accompanied by horrible gestures and facial contortions, or making animal sounds, is a certain sign of demon spirits. The Holy Spirit may be authoritative or sad or grieving in the messages He brings the Body through the gifts, but He is never condemnatory in tone, nor does He bring fear. (Awe and reverence of God, the "fear of the Lord," is not like a "spirit of fear," which He does not give us (Rom. 8:15, 2 Tim. 1:7).

Someone from a noted Bible school recently came to "check out" one of our services and got up and left halfway through the meeting. His reason was that "something began to stir around inside me, so this ministry must be in error." What really happened was that he apparently *needed* deliverance, and the spirits oppressing him began to move around in discomfort. The Holy Spirit would have "peaceably" given him a witness, or a "knowing," that the doctrine we preached was in error or would have shown him through discernment of spirits if the spirit behind us was satanic. The Holy Spirit does not "stir around" in discomfort and try to impel a person to leave a service. He makes a quiet suggestion or Word or witness, but does not try to push the person into complying. He is a gentleman and respects our free will—even when we are wrong. The choice or decision is always ours.

A witness of the Holy Spirit, for example, is the best way to check on dolls, stuffed animals, or art works that are not obviously accursed things, as well as on attitudes toward real animals. An inordinate attraction to, or preoccupation with, any of these things, of course, is evidence that something is wrong, but only knowledge from the Holy Spirit will show you if a demon is present. In either case, the ungodly soul tie must be broken.) One family recently featured in nationwide newspaper stories collects teddy bears, which many people do. The difference is that this family was obsessed with bears. They had seats at the table for five or six "chief bears"; they took many of the bears with them on vacations or even short trips; they took them to sit in the living room, and they put them to bed like children. Other things in the newspaper stories made it very clear these people not only had ungodly soul ties to the stuffed animals but an entire tribe of demons were being housed in the teddy bears!

Occult Sins and Deliverance

Occult simply means "something hidden" from plain sight. Participation in any occult practices, including apparently harmless groups who do a lot of "good" in the world, results in wounds to the spirit. John Sandford says:

> Involvement in occultism is like forcing a lovely soprano voice to sing bass. That harms the vocal cords . . . Sin, especially occultism, destroys the wholesome flow of the spirit in action to the body.[1]

Of "harmless" or "for fun" involvements, he says:

> However innocuous it may seem, sin is sin, and sets in motion forces that must be dealt with in one way or another

... God is compassionate (see Ps. 103) ... But the laws of the universe are neither compassionate nor indulgent ... just as the law of gravity cannot be denied, neither can God revoke His laws because foolish children do not understand ... Results from one instance of occult activity in childhood may afflict someone horribly in adulthood ... Dabblers in the occult do not generally immediately reap what they have sown, but it is inevitable that one day they will.[2]

Complete deliverance involves true repentance—renunciation of these things as sin—casting out of demons, and healing of these wounds to the spirit; in other words, the entire ministry of sanctification as it has been given to us. These transgressions involve the actual partaking of things of the enemy and actively assisting his cause. Man's spirit, made in the image of God, cannot help but be wounded or even distorted (mutated) by the committing of spiritual sins—"pride of life" sins, not just "the lust of the eyes" (soulish) and the "lust of the flesh" (body).

People are drawn into these things by a feeling of superiority, or pride, that leads them into a search of forbidden or occult knowledge and then into having power over the events in their own lives, nature, and other people. In other words, they knowingly or through deception allow Satan to trigger the **ye shall be as gods** motive in them just as he did in Eve in the Garden of Eden. Pride was Satan's downfall originally, and all mankind inherits that sin in one form or another from Adam and Eve's contamination. Until we are born again, Satan is our father. We "inherit" his characteristics through heredity or environment. In spite of a new spirit, most Christians still operate out of that "sin-consciousness" programmed into the memory banks (robotmind) of their souls.

Deliverance did not end with the apostles. Early church history shows examples of casting out demons just as it shows examples of the ministries of the gifts of the Holy Spirit in operation. One such report is in the writings of Theophilus in the second century:

> . . . Those who are possessed by demons are sometimes exorcized in the name of the real God, and the deceiving spirits themselves confess that they are the demons who were also at work at that time in the poets (the Greek writers Homer and Hesiod).[3]

No matter how inspired some teachings seem or how good they sound, if they do not uphold *the same Jesus* of the Bible and His teachings, they are satanic. This is equally true in the fields of religion, literature, entertainment, and education. The Twentieth Century might be labeled, "the Age of Deception," because so much satanic deception has become an accepted part of society in all fields. Listed below are organizations that are occult or have occult influences, although their stated aims and purposes may be "good." People need deliverance after participating in these groups as much as after participation in false religions and cults.

Occult-Influenced Groups

1. *Mormonism*—among other things, it preaches "another Jesus" than the one in the Bible.

2. *Freemasonry*—involves secret rites and is a revival of pagan worship of the sun god Osiris, Mithras, Bacchus, Dionysius, Atys, and so forth. In other words, it substitutes Satan for Jesus—the sun god for the *Son* God. Initiates are required to swear allegiance to this other god. "Upper chamber" lodge meetings to "worship celestial bodies" are a disguised form of worship of Baal or Moloch, the Greek Tyrian Hercules, known to Masons as the "Tyrian architect." People who have been Masons or members of the auxiliary organizations always need deliverance just as people who have been involved in astrology or spiritualism.

How to Tell the True From the False 65

3. *Psychic organizations*—Spiritual Frontiers Fellowship, Association for Research and Enlightment (Edgar Cayce), and other New Age organizations, Rosicrucianism, and Astara.

4. *Scouting*—This will shock most people until they investigate the American Indian religious background built into the organization. Children are taught ceremonies and dances (which were originally dedicated to various gods, or demons); Indian totems which elevate certain animals to tribal gods—bears, coyotes, wolves, and so forth; symbolic lodges and medicine men; self-reliance rather than reliance on God; stargazing and magic through Indian lore; and many other such things.

The main organizations that sponsor Scouts are churches, although Scouting teaches many unscriptural things, such as that all religions are good. Many false religions are promoted as well as Christianity. The "brotherhood" of *all* people is stressed, and leaders are admonished not to neglect the boys for "among them may be the one who will grow up to lead the world to peace."[4]

5. *Roman Catholicism*—more and more Catholics are becoming born again and filled with the Spirit, but the fact remains that many of the church's doctrines are not only heresies but involve occultism. Some people operating in deliverance have found that past involvement with this religion for some people means demonic oppression. The person's attitude toward rosaries, praying to saints, the Mass, and so forth, seems to be the key factor. If the person has made an idol out of artifacts or actually worshipped dead human beings, then that person needs deliverance.

The purpose of this book is not to stress demons, but freedom from demons or sanctification/deliverance. However, one must have some understanding of how Satan operates in order to understand sanctification. So we are going to discuss his kingdom next.

End Notes

1. Sandford, *Healing the Wounded Spirit*, pp. 298, 299.
2. Ibid., p. 300.
3. Robert M. Grant (text and translation), *Theophilus of Antioch Ad Autolycum*, (England: London, Oxford University Press, 1970), Book II.8, p. 39.
4. Worley, The Battle Royal: I, p. 114.

8
The Unholy Trinity

We sometimes act as if other people were our enemies, but the apostle Paul said:

> **For we wrestle not against flesh and blood, but against principalities, against powers, against the rulers of darkness of this world, against spiritual wickedness in high places.**
>
> Ephesians 6:12

Satan was the highest created being until pride brought him down. (Isa. 14:12-14; Ez. 28:11-15.) Most Christians refer to him as an "archangel," but only one archangel is mentioned. That is Michael in Jude 9. And only one other angelic being is mentioned by name in the entire Bible. That is *Gabriel*, who was named in Daniel 8:16 and 9:21 and in Luke 1:19 and 26. In Scripture, Satan is referred to as **the anointed cherub that covereth** (Eze. 28:14), so apparently he was a cherubim and possibly a different order of being. However, some Bible scholars think *cherubim* are simply a higher order of angels. (For a description of their appearance, read Ezekiel 10 and 11.)

One purpose of cherubim was to provide a *covering* (security)—for the gates of Eden and for the mercy seat in the Holy of Holies and the indwelling of the Holy Spirit there. (Ex. 25:22.) Satan was the **covering cherub on the mountain of God** (Eze. 26:14), and he took a third of the angels with him in his fall. (Luke 10:18, Rev. 12:4.)

Among other things, Satan is called the **prince of this world** (John 16:11), ruler of an evil world order of men and fallen beings; the **prince of the power of the air** (Eph. 2:2), ruler of the atmosphere, or the Second Heaven; and the **god of this age** (2 Cor. 4:4), who rules secular philosophies, as well as false religions.

He is not self-existent, having been created, and he is not all-powerful, all-knowing, or ever-present. To rule his systems and subvert humanity, he must rely on fallen beings under his authority. His chain of command is copied from God's. Satan was not created in the image of God; therefore, he does not have the ability to create—only to copy, pervert, and subvert, to mimic and seduce and deceive. He is the "father of lies" (John 8:44), the father of deception.

The *Holy Trinity* is: God the Father, God the Son, and God the Holy Spirit. From our research and from knowledge gained through deliverance of many people, we have seen that Satan also has a ruling "trinity": the principalities of Antichrist, Death and Hades, and the Queen of Heaven, or Jezebel. A principality rules over a territory as large as a nation or as small as a person. Apparently, principalities also rule systems, such as economic, political, and educational.

Principalities of Satan

I. *Antichrist Principality:* People think of Antichrist as the man through whom Satan will rule the earth in the end times or as "anti-God" philosophies and religions. However, the only places where the word is mentioned in Scripture are the books of 1 and 2 John. If you read those carefully, you will see that John's problem with the **many antichrists** who had come (1 John 2:18) was not so much false teaching *as the questioning of his own authority* (1 John 2:24). Travis Walters says in *He Who Laughs in the Heavens:*

> Those who were manifesting antichrist were not abiding in what they heard from the beginning. Why weren't they? *Because they believed that they were as capable of hearing God as was John* . . . so they gave themselves over to seducing spirits. The deception began when they determined to rebel against the authority of the Apostle John. *The spirit of antichrist is primarily* (first of all) *the spirit of rebellion!*

An interesting fact is that rebellion does not become obvious until confronted by authority. In a church where there is little or no scriptural emphasis on submission, rebellion can reign almost unnoticed (although it still does its destructive work). But begin to bring in teaching concerning divine order, and every antichrist spirit in the place will sooner or later raise its ugly head.[1]

A. *Characteristics*—These demons influence men to usurp authority. They instigate and instill self-will and rebellion. They turn sons against fathers, employees against bosses, church members or even ministry staff members against a pastor or head of ministry. In the public arena, they set citizens against police. Today, members of Congress are trying to usurp the powers of the executive branch and make foreign policy. For a classic Biblical example, see the story of the Korah rebellion against Moses. (Numbers 16.)

One indication of this spirit is when a person, who *knows* to what position he has been assigned, begins to look at those over him and feel he is "just as good." He will think, and then begin to say, "My plan or preaching or leadership is just as good as his." Then he will begin to say, "I can preach or lead or whatever *better* than he can. I should be on top."

At that time, he has started to listen to, if not house, a "top dog" (antichrist) spirit. Even if the Holy Spirit shows this man where he belongs and what he is to do, he will think, "I should be at the top!" He is becoming unteachable and is following Satan: **I will ascend to Heaven, I will exalt my throne above the stars of God . . . I will make myself like the Most High** (Isa. 14:13,14).

A man oppressed by an antichrist spirit believes he does not need to submit to anyone else's authority —but demands absolute obedience from those under him. These spirits promote independence and work against submission. Also, someone in *spoken* submission may not be in *actual* submission. If someone claims to be submitted to a pastor's authority, yet questions every decision and immediately suggests alternate plans, he may not just be argumentative. He may be showing the presence of an antichrist spirit. Many pastoral staff members operate under an "Absalom" spirit. Sooner or later, they attempt to take some of the members and start another church. They have no concept or understanding of the meaning of true *submission*.

One of the best books on divine authority is Watchman Nee's *Spiritual Authority*. He said:

1. *Obedience* is related to conduct: it is relative. *Submission* is related to heart attitude: it is absolute.
2. God alone receives unqualified obedience without measure; any person lower than God can only receive qualified obedience.
3. Should the delegated authority issue an order clearly contradicting God's command, he will be given submission but not obedience. We should submit to the *person* who has received delegated authority from God, but we should disobey the order which offends God.[2]

An antichrist spirit over a man will push him to find a woman (or in some cases, another man) operating under a Jezebel spirit to work with, although he does not usually marry a woman like this. Antichrist-influenced men tend to marry women who are "door mats." Women with Jezebel spirits tend to marry "Ahab" (wimpy) men, but they team up in churches with antichrist men. Her role is to help him build his "kingdom." Both man and woman are unsubmissive which allows them to come under the control of spirits who influence the usurpation of authority from properly constituted leadership. These liaisons *can* have strong sexual overtones and lead to adultery. If these two did end up getting married, you would begin to see a strong spirit of competition enter into the relationship. *An important thing to remember is: oppression by these kinds of spirits is possible because of the wrong attitude of the heart.*

The Bible adds another characteristic of the antichrist spirit: to revile the glorious ones. (Jude 9,10.) Apparently, these are fallen angels. The comparable passage in 2 Peter is: 2:11

> . . . them that walk after the flesh in the lust of uncleanness, and despise government. Presumptuous are they, selfwilled, they are not afraid to speak evil of dignities. Whereas angels, (glorious ones) which are greater in power and might, bring not railing accusation against them before the Lord.
>
> 2 Peter 2:10,11

    Even those in deliverance ministries should not taunt demons or boast over them. Jesus told the disciples not to rejoice because of their authority over demons, but rather to rejoice over their own salvation. (Luke 10:20.) Peter was saying people who hate authority have enough pride to make fun of supernatural beings.

  B. *Cords or chains by which these spirits bind men*—rebellion, self-will, and pride, or the "kingdom of self," which includes all the "self" attitudes from self-love to self-hate.

II. *Death and Hades Principalities:* (Mt. 16:18,19; John 10:10; Rev. 20:13,14.)

  A. *Characteristics*—Jesus said in Matthew 16:18:

> **And I tell you that you are Peter, and on this rock I will build my church, and** *the gates of hell* **will not overcome it.** NIV

Hell in this verse from the *King James Version* is really the Greek word hades and "gates" in the Bible stands for ruling power. Therefore, when the Church exercises *its* authority properly, the strong man of hades will be robbed of his power and ability to keep people in spiritual prisons or to take them to early graves. Sinners in the grasp of Death and Hades spirits commit immorality and murder and follow their instincts to destroy and rebel. They are not afraid of the kingdom of darkness and are covetous, selfish, empty, restless, and full of

The Unholy Trinity

shame. They are malcontents, boasters who flatter people to gain advantage, and grumblers. (Rom. 1, 2 Tim. 3.)

Revelation 6:8 says *Death* rode a pale horse, **and Hell** (hades) **followed with him,** or "death with hades following." *As a church binds "death with hades following," the lost will have their ears unstopped so they can at least hear the Gospel.* It releases them to experience miracles and healings. All will not believe or accept, but they will be able to hear. At present, many who would believe cannot hear *because of death and hades principalities.*

These demons afflict Christians with physical infirmities, doubts, fears, and lusts of the world (worldliness). Ministries of healing and miracles are blocked by these spirits.

B. *Cords by which these spirits bind men*—birth traumas, accidents, grief over tragedies, and occult participation or curses in the bloodline which allow a spirit of death to enter. These spirits bring in self-destruction (overeating, overdrinking, overworking) or suicidal tendencies, infirmities (similar to death spirits but their job is to weaken the body so disease can enter), abortion, fear of death or the unknown, tiredness or fatigue or weakness, and even famine, hunger, and massive poverty. From Revelation 6:1-8, it appears that one of the primary functions of Death and Hades is to bring pestilence and destruction.

III. *Queen Mother, or Jezebel Principality:* (1 Kings 16:31, chapters 18-21; 2 Kings 9; Isaiah 47:1,10; Rev. 2:18-25, 17:1-19, 18:4,8.)

A. *Characteristics*—not those usually associated in our minds with the word *Jezebel.* Satan has caused the word to be defined only in sexually enticing ways (cosmetics, revealing fashions, and seductive behavior) to cover up "Jezebel's" other activities. This principality is not female at all but is called by the name of the woman in the Bible who personifies its heathen worship character and operations. For purposes of clarity, we will call it "she" or "her."

The Jezebel of 1 and 2 Kings is not described as a seductive woman but as a *usurping* woman. She was a priestess of Baal and fed Baal's prophets at her table. She had many prophets of God killed and sought to slay Elijah. She was ruthless and **wrote letters in Ahab's name** (1 Kings 21:8) that by subterfuge and murder gained him the vineyard he coveted. She stirred up wickedness in the sight of the Lord and caused Ahab to follow idols, and she subverted other nations by marrying her daughter to the future king of the Nation of Judah and causing that nation to sin. She outlived her husband many years and Elijah some years. Finally, she was killed after a prophet anointed Jehu to take the kingdom from Ahab's son Joram. (Women afflicted with Jezebelic spirits usually outlive their husbands by many years.)

The only place where the modern definition of Jezebel has any basis is one verse: **she painted her face, and tired her head,** (did her hair) **and looked out at a window** (2 Kings 9:30), and those actions were not for the purpose of seduction but in a desperate attempt to maintain her power and authority over the Nation of Israel. Her husband was gone, and her sons were gone, but she sought to remain *"the power behind the throne."* That is the real character of the Jezebel personality: the power behind the throne, or women who rule through puppet-men. However, she assigns and dispatches spirits of sexual lust. (See below.)

B. Revelation 2:18-25 shows *five things for which Jezebel in the heavenlies is responsible.*

1. She calls herself a *prophetess*. Most demons who operate in the field of religion are subject to the Jezebel principality. This includes all kind of traditions (Matt. 7:8,9,13; Gal. 1:14, 3:10; Col. 2:8; and James 2:8-13), cultural as well as religious. This attitude is manifested as "What was good enough for mother and father," and similar comments. Traditional and religious spirits—powers under Jezebel—include those over all kinds of false teaching, false doctrines, Pharisaism (legalism), cults, and humanism (the religion that elevates man over God).

   Walters wrote, concerning tradition, that the Lord spoke this to him:

   Tradition is more than just a demon within a few persons—it is a power in the heavenlies. The power of Tradition is what has shipwrecked the modern Pentecostal movement.[3]

   What are some examples of religious tradition in our society? Perhaps the best way to answer this is to make a partial list: Sunday School at 9:30 or 9:45; church buildings; pews facing the front; hymn books; Sunday night church; the order of service . . . printed bulletins; robed choirs and ministers; sitting, standing, or kneeling at appointed times; the altar call; Wednesday night prayer meeting. The strong man of tradition subtly brings people to believe that these things are sacred in and of themselves . . . whereas the truth of the matter is that none of the above-mentioned items is vital to knowing or pleasing God. All of them can be instituted or disposed with as the Spirit so leads. We need to bind the power of tradition so that we can hear what the Spirit is telling us to keep and what He is telling us to change or shelve![4]

The discussion of tradition in Colossians 2:8,16,17,20-23 shows two things: tradition indulges the flesh (v. 23) while the **substance belongs to Christ** (v. 17). Following "habits of worship" or tradition tends to pull us away from seeking the Holy Spirit constantly and consistently as to what He wants in each service.

2. She *teaches and beguiles* God's servants (manipulative witchcraft which we call "jezebelic"). This is the "cord" through which usurpation-of-male-authority spirits work.
3. She teaches the practice of *immorality*. Spirits assigned to trigger sexual lusts and perversions are under her authority.
4. She encourages the eating of *food that has been sacrificed, or dedicated, to idols* (Satan). That means these spirits promote a light or permissive attitude toward sin. They project images of "sloppy agape," of God as a permissive mother who allows love for the children to override the need for discipline (which really is a perversion of love that results in spoiled, or "rotten," children). Jezebel promotes unconditional acceptance of the sin, not just the sinner. The "brotherhood of all men" is a jezebelic philosophy.

God's true character is to love through discipline, not without it. Real father love is expressed in correction and instruction that causes a child to grow up straight and not warped. He sets standards and expects obedience. In the Bible, God says, "I love mankind, but if they persist in sin, I will put them away from Me."

The father of the Prodigal Son did not follow him into the pig pen saying, "That's all right. I'll help you. You couldn't help being this way. You had to express yourself to find out who you are."

The father did not make a move toward the son *until* the youth repented, changed his ways, and came home. *Then* the father ran to meet him in love. God *loves* all of the people in the world, but they are not His children unless they accept Jesus. God loves all of His children, but He will not condone their misbehavior. After a period of time (which He alone determines) during which the Holy Spirit corrects and instructs, God moves in discipline or judgment. The Church is being judged today because of having become permeated with so much jezebelic influence that most Christians believe anything is all right "because God loves us." Consequently, many believers today are "eating food sacrificed to idols," or participating in things God has forbidden, such as astrology.

5. She teaches the "deep things of Satan," or occult knowledge.

Jezebel of the Old Testament sought to slay the prophets of God and promoted the religion of Satan. Today jezebelic spirits operate no differently. If they cannot kill ministers, they seek to "kill" their voice in the Church through one means or another. If they cannot entice ministers into immorality, false teachings, or occultism, they seek to "kill" them through persecution or ridicule. The Jezebelic person will "kill" or try to kill the anointing on an apostle or a prophet of God. This can keep him from seeing salvations, healings, or mir-

acles. The purpose is to stifle the prophetic voices of God and substitute false voices.
C. *Other consequences of Jezebel influence*—in Revelation 17 and 18, Jezebel is called Babylon. Referring back to Babylon in Isaiah 47:6-13, we see the pollution of God's people, but we also see other things for which this principality is responsible. They are:
1. *The problems of old age*—**on the aged you laid a very heavy yoke** NIV (v.6). This means growing old is made harder than it should be even after the fall. *Problems of old age* today range from economic (no respect for older people in the marketplace anymore) to abuse of the elderly (caused by contempt of age, a companion of the exaltation of youth since World War II) to new diseases of senility. Alzheimer's Disease is a jezebelic spirit.
2. *Drug abuse*—**the multitude of thy sorceries** (v. 9). Jezebel certainly is having a field day now with "sorceries!"
3. *Witchcraft*—**the great power of your enchantments** RSV (v. 9), and *astrology* (v. 13), the New Age movement and the occult "explosion" that has occurred since the Sixties.
4. *Hedonism* (the pursuit of fleshly pleasures)—**you lover of pleasures** RSV (v. 8). This includes "eating, drinking, and making merry" as in the days of Noah—self-indulgence and laziness. This country, since World War II, has grown increasingly addicted to illicit sexual pleasures, food and drink, and recreation and games. We need to eat and drink and have a certain amount of relaxation, of course, but the jezeblic influence in America has made gluttony, illicit and perverse sex, and sports and recreation a way of life.

5. *Fear*—**if so be thou mayst prevail** (v. 12). The word translated *prevail* in the *King James Version* usually is used in connection with God moving in judgment. Here it means this principality may bring fear on mankind.

**Perhaps you will succeed,
Perhaps you will cause terror.** (NIV)

Today, fear in all of its aspects is said to be "pandemic." Newspapers and medical journals contain articles concerning people with successful lives and no problems who suddenly had "something come over them." Eventually, they were institutionalized because of one kind of fear or another. The fact is that a jezebelic spirit jumped on them. Many other people are oppressed by fears of nuclear war or environmental disasters.

Author-teacher Don Basham says God showed him a vision of the American bureaucracy under the authority and power of the Jezebel principality. He described the spirit as "octopus-like" with tentacles going everywhere,[5] (also a typical description of a possessive and permissive mother). The civil servants are the people who really run America. We cannot do anything without running into the "red tape" (tentacles) of the bureaucracy (agencies and administrations) that many times usurps the authority of the governing bodies.

D. The *cords* of the Queen Mother include the five things listed above as her primary activities: religion and tradition; occultism; sexual perversions and lust; the permissive mother attitude; and witchcraft—control spirits of false security, peace, defensive shields, divorce (home-wrecking and church-wrecking spirits), and false personalities (schizophrenia).[6]

Because of the "Babylon" references, the Jezebel principality apparently is the Queen of Heaven known since ancient times. This cult began with Semiramis, the wife of Nimrod, who had been raised from the common people to become queen. After her husband died a horrible death (torn to pieces), she set him up to be worshipped as a god. To perpetuate her power and authority, she perverted God's words about a coming **Seed** (Gen. 3:15) and said her dead husband had mystically impregnated her with the "divinely promised seed" and was reincarnated as the child Tammuz! "Thus the great launching of the mystery religion of Babylon," Winkie Pratney writes.[7]

This is the source of the deification of the "Queen of Heaven" (Jer. 44:25) and her child and the sun god — her husband, called by other names in Roman, Greek, and other nations' myths and legends. She is the prototype of Mother Nature: "the Mother Archetype" whose strengths are those of a mother's care and sympathy, but who "presides over the place of magic, transformation and rebirth together with the underworld and its inhabitants" and "anything secret, hidden, dark, the abyss, the world of the dead, anything that devours, seduces, and poisons, that is terrifying and inescapable like fate"[8]

Semiramis soon became the favorite object of worship in the ancient world and is known as Aphrodite and Venus, as well. At the fall of Babylon, her priests fled to Pergamos—called the place "where the seat of Satan is" (Rev. 2:13)—and later to Italy where they adopted tall, pointed hats in honor of the fish god. Pratney says Babylon is a *"supernatural pattern,*

The Unholy Trinity

"a demonic structure that even now profoundly influences the entire world."[9] He says the worship of the "goddess-mother" (the Jezebel principality) goes on today in *open witchcraft* and the "hidden spirtual power base of the religious but anti-Christian section of the *feminist movement.*"[10]

Under this *unholy trinity* of principalities are many other "families" of spirits with which we come into contact during our sanctification sessions.

End Notes

1. Walters, *He Who Laughs in the Heavens*, pp. 54, 56.
2. Watchman Nee, *Spiritual Authority*, p. 109.
3. Walters, p. 46.
4. Ibid., p. 47.
5. Don Basham, "Jezebel Over America," Cassette tape *DT094*, available from Integrity Communications, P. O. Z, Mobile, AL 36616.
6. The world's psychological *schizophrenia* is really demon possession of the spirit of a person. "Satan" literally has entered into that person, and he has become "mad." The spiritual definition that we use is "double-mindedness," or literally having two souls, a false one (or a demon) or two demonic false souls that squeeze the person's real soul between them so that it has little or no expression of its own. This person's spirit may be saved and even filled with the Holy Spirit, but his personality is under the control of demons. (See Frank Hammond's *Pigs in the Parlor.*)
7., 8., 9., 10. Winkie Pratney, *Devil Take the Youngest* (Louisiana: Shreveport, Huntington House Inc., 1985), pp. 23-28, p. 31, p. 28, p. 57.

9
The Authority of the Believer

Satan has principalities and powers, and hordes of demons, but his authority has been taken away! (Luke 10:17-19.) He is a defeated foe. In other words, he still has a certain amount of power through what we allow in our own lives and through his lordship over the world systems and orders. *However, his authority has been taken away by Jesus.* An analogy is the American Civil War:

After the slaves were emancipated by Abraham Lincoln, there still remained the battles to "dethrone" the Confederate powers and to retake the territory for the United States. Those leaders and generals still had some power, but their authority over the slaves had been taken away.

What remains for the Church today is to take territory back from Satan, to "spoil" his house, and to remain victorious over all of our enemies. How do we do that? Through the *blood of Jesus and the word of our testimony.* (Rev. 12:11.) The *saints* (elect) of God now have the authority over Satan. He no longer has any rightful authority over us, although his demons still harass and afflict and try to defeat us individually any time they find an opening.

The Greek word *euaggelion,* translated the *gospel,* which was to be preached to all the inhabited world means "good news."

- The Good News is not "shape up or ship out."
- The Good News is not "God is going to get you."
- The Good News is that *God has solved the sin problem!*

The "good news" of Christ is Satan's defeat: The world no longer has to remain in slavery.

Many Christians, however, because of traditional doctrines or lack of knowledge have their freedom *but remain in slavery to the power of Satan*—which is absolutely unnecessary!

Divine Order

God is an orderly Being. He does nothing on whim, but according to His principles. We do not always see His reasons because **His ways are higher than our ways** (Isa. 55:8,9); nevertheless, we can bank on the fact that His reasons are there and that they are good. *Divine order* means the pattern, principles, and purposes of God.

The Father delegated *all authority* to His Son, the Lord Jesus Christ. (Matt. 28:18.) He is the Lord of all creation, but while He is sitting at the right hand of the Father, we are His ambassadors in the earth. God wants His children to have a part in the occupying and reclaiming of territory that Jesus won from the "god of this world" at Calvary. Jesus is the Head, but He must have a physical Body on earth to spread the "good news" of what He did to destroy the works of Satan. He is the Head that gives directions through the Holy Spirit, and we are the Body that *should be* carrying out those directions. (Eph. 1:18-23, Eph. 3:17-33; Col. 2:19.)

Jesus has set up patterns of authority, or chains of command, within the Body as well. He begins with the five-fold

The Authority of the Believer

ministries, which He sets within the Body as "gifts" to help the other members accomplish their missions. These "gifts" are the apostles, prophets, evangelists, pastors, and teachers. (Eph. 4:11.) We are to honor these *offices* more than we would honor the office of President of the United States. The way to tell true or false ministers is to judge the fruit and discern the person (through the Spirit). We are not to honor the person because of looks, oratory, great knowledge, or fame, but we are to honor him as a representative of Jesus.

The people serving in the five ministry offices have been chosen by Jesus and delegated *His own* authority with which to administrate in the Church. *To accept or reject the delegate, or ambassador, is to accept or reject the One Who sent him.* A *delegate* is "someone who represents, or acts for, someone else."

The teaching of the *authority of the believer* has been misunderstood and misinterpreted very badly in many areas. The *believer* only has authority over the devil and his works: demons, sickness and disease, poverty, and the other consequences of curses which are the devil's works. We only have that because of, and through, Jesus. In ourselves, we have no authority. The believer does *not* have authority over other believers or over their wills (that constitutes witchcraft).

Believers who are members of local bodies, even those who are elders and deacons or operate in ministries of helps, do *not* have authority over—or even equal to—the five-fold offices. This particular misunderstanding is one which has allowed many religious spirits, many demons of pride and self-will, and even antichrist and Jezebel spirits to operate in churches.

Many have missed the point that the nine ministries Paul listed in 1 Corinthians 12:8-11 are gifts of the Holy Spirit *for* the Body. A believer who operates in one or more of those gifts does not *have* the gift. He is to *administer* the gift to the Body. The gift is *to* the Body, not to the person who ministers it. No one has the "gift of prophecy" or the "gift of miracles" or the "gift of the word of wisdom." The Holy Spirit has the "gifts." Certain believers, selected only by the Holy Spirit (1 Cor. 12:11), are called by Him to operate His gifts for the benefit of the Body.

The main purpose of the gifts of the Holy Spirit are to edify the Church (1 Cor. 14:5, Eph. 4:12). They are for the Body of Christ, although the operator of the gifts may also be edified as a result.

The Holy Spirit was sent by Jesus to comfort, counsel, and teach. His role is to assist and empower every member of the Body who will allow Him, *not to rule the Church*. The government of the Church is on the shoulders of Jesus through His five-fold ministries. The Holy Spirit's role is to uphold and show forth Jesus, the Authority, the Supreme Ruler, the Lord of lords and King of kings. Most Charismatics believe that because they operate in the ministry of the gift of prophecy, they are *equal in authority* to the pastor and prophet—and that is not Biblically sound. That is a "tradition" of man. If persisted in, that false idea can lead to rebellion against Jesus' appointed authority, to pride in oneself, and to the usurpation of true authority. An "Absalom spirit" is an operation of the Antichrist principality.[1]

Saying, "I shall be like him (the pastor or other five-fold ministry office holder)" or "I have as much right as he does to say what shall be done" is the same sin Satan committed against God and Absalom committed against David. Pride brings self-will, and rebellion is as witchcraft (1 Sam. 15:23), no matter who commits it.

The holder of the five-fold office must judge his own attitudes and behavior. He must know that proper use of his authority under Jesus constitutes feeding and serving the sheep under him. He is called to be a servant, to love the people sent to him as Jesus loves them. Those in the five-fold offices are

The Authority of the Believer 87

not called to be tyrants. Intimidation, manipulation, and exploitation are not aspects of Godly authority but signs of soul power.[2] God's divine order and the authority of Jesus is never to be enforced. The authority of Jesus does not consist of *making* believers obey, but of being such an example to them that they *want* to follow the minister's leading.

The believer has authority over the devil, his cohorts, and all of their works, but he is *under* authority in the Church. One who has been called to operate in the gifts of the Holy Spirit is *under* and subject to the authority of one of the five-fold offices. Every believer, no matter what his calling, should seek God as to the local body of which he should be a part, then he should not leave that local body—*no matter what happens*—until he is given a witness from the Lord to move.

Other delineations of God's divine order on earth are:
a. Order in the Church—Timothy 1:4-16, 3:9-11.
b. Order in congregational services—1 Corinthians 14:23-40.
c. Order in Church families—Ephesians 5:22-6:4.
d. Order in the lives of members of the Body—Titus 2, 3:1-8.
e. Order in the ordinances of the Church—1 Corinthians 11:23-30.
f. Order in the collection of finances—1 Corinthians 16:1,2.
g. Order between husbands and wives in the Body—I Corinthians 11:3; Ephesians 5:22-33.
h. Order between parents and children—Ephesians 6:1-4.

God's "chain of command," or His divine order among believers is channeled according to this pattern: Jesus, man, woman, children. In the Church, the pattern is: Jesus, five-fold offices, believers. Deacons, elders, and ministries of helps are *not* Biblical authority positions, although they may be administrative positions under a five-fold office and operate in delegated authority from that office. They are *appointed to help or assist the authority office* in serving the Body and in carrying out the ministry.

What Is Authority?

Authority, according to one dictionary definition, is "the right to give orders" or "to take specific action."[3] One scholar says the Greek words *exesti* and *exousia* (used most often in the New Testament for "authority") combine the two ideas of right and might. The same scholar says:

> *Exousia* denotes the executive power while *arche* (rule) represents the authority granting the power (Lk. 20:20). The combined meaning of right and might is indicated in Jn. 5:27; 17:2; 19:10,11. *Exousia* also means justified, rightly supra-ordinated power (Mt. 8:9; Rev. 18:1). In 1 Cor. 11:10, it is clear from the connection in vv. 6,7 that authority on the head is the same as covering on the head. . . .[4]

Authority also is a covering. As used in the Bible, covering has many aspects. It can mean "protection" or a shelter ("a refuge"), or "security," or even "balance." Satan as a cherubim had the responsibility to be a *covering*. A husband's authority is to be a *covering* for his wife. Parental authority is a *covering* for children. Pastoral authority is a *covering* for the sheep. As an undershepherd appointed to authority by the Chief Shepherd, a pastor (or any other of the five-fold offices) has the responsibility of *covering* any sheep who come under his administration.

Various mentions of *coverings* in Scripture include:

1. "The blood of a lamb" and the "cloud" for the Israelites. (Ex. 12 and Ps. 105:39.)
2. "The garments of salvation" for individual believers. (Isa. 52:1-3, 61:10; Esther 5:1-3; Ps. 45:13; and Rom. 13:14.)
3. Jesus as a covering for the Body universal as its members speak the same thing and are submitted to one another in the love and fear of God. (Eph. 5:21.)

The Authority of the Believer

4. The cherubim as a covering for the mercy seat and the veil for the Holy of Holies. (Ex. 25:17-21, 26:33.)
5. Proper principles of prayer, praise, and worship constitute a covering for entering into the presence of God. (Lev. 16:11-13.)

Therefore one thing *authority* means is "responsibility" for certain duties or certain territories. Several Greek verbs are used in the New Testament for aspects of *ruling over* or taking responsibility for certain areas:

1. *Reign*—"to rule over in the sense of power and principality, to be first" (Rom. 15:12).
2. *Guide*—"*to take charge of a household*" (1 Tim. 5:14).
3. *Rule*—"to lead, maintain, stand before, or attend with care and diligence" (Rom. 12:8, 1 Tim. 3:4,5,12 and 5:17).
4. *Feed*—"*the whole office of a shepherd; tending, feeding, and protecting flocks; putting of the flock into folds*" (Mt. 2:6, Luke 17:7, John 21:16, Acts 20:28, 1 Cor. 9:7, 1 Pet. 5:2, Jude 12, Rev. 2:27).
5. *Rule* (in a different sense than #3)—"to act as an umpire, to arbitrate, decide, or direct" (Col. 3:15).

Being *in* authority or *under* authority requires an attitude of submission. The opposite of *submission*, of course, is *rebellion*. The primary Hebrew root word for rebellion is *marah* which means "bitterness" or "to be made bitter," "to rebel," or "to resist." Rebellion is resistance to, or defiance of, authority. This attitude seems to be the prevailing hindrance to unity in the Body. Since the 1960s, we have been living in a rebellious society. Someone in a state of rebellion against constituted authority is *not* sanctified.

Basic Purposes of Authority

When Paul wrote that resisting civil authority is resisting the ordinances of God, he meant more than is at first visible.

> Let every soul be subject unto the higher powers. For there is no power but of God: the powers that be are ordained of God.
>
> Whosoever therefore resisteth the power, resisteth the ordinance of God: and they that resist shall receive to themselves damnation.
>
> Romans 13:1-7

Paul was talking of earthly governments, but these verses embody in intent the basic purpose of being under authority:

— To grow in wisdom and character. Jesus submitted to the authority of his parents at age 12 when they found him "going about" His Father's business. And the Bible says He **increased in wisdom and stature, and in favor with God and man** (Luke 2:52).

— To gain protection from destructive temptations. The idea of submitting is not to get under domination, but to get under protection. Being "lone rangers" leaves us exposed to unnecessary temptations that may be too strong for us to overcome. This is why *rebellion* is akin to *witchcraft* (1 Sam. 15:23). Both terms mean subjecting oneself to the realm and power of Satan.

— To receive clear direction for decisions in one's life. One aspect of faith many Christians miss is faith that God will give instruction and general direction through those placed over us.

Scriptures on the authority structure of the *family* (father, mother, children) are 1 Corinthians 11:10, Ephesians 6:22, Colossians 3:20, Ephesians 6:1-3, Proverbs 6:20,21, 15:5, and 30:17.

Scriptures concerning governmental authority structures are 1 Peter 2:13,14, Romans 13:1-7.

Scriptures concerning Church authority are 1 Thessalonians 5:12,13, Hebrews 13:17, 1 Timothy 5:17,18, and 1 Peter 5:1-3.

Scriptures concerning authority in business are Colossians 3:22-24, 1 Timothy 6:1,2.

> . . . These things teach and exhort. If any man teach otherwise . . . He is proud, knowing nothing.
>
> 1 Timothy 6:2-4

Jesus' authority delegated to believers *not* in a fivefold office means only three things: the responsibility for witnessing (preaching) to those of the world, the responsibility to operate with "signs and wonders (practical ministry) following," and responsibility for casting out of demons (authority over the devil) from other people and from their own affairs and lives. (Mark 11:17-23.) The Holy Spirit's operation of any of His nine gifts through believers not set in a fivefold office is *not* to give them authority in the Church but to empower or assist them in the three areas where they do have responsibility.

End Notes

1. Dr. Mark T. Barclay, *Beware of Seducing Spirits,* Mark Barclay Publications, P. O. Box 584, Midland, Michigan 48640.
2. Randy Shankle, *The Merismos,* (Oklahoma: Tulsa, Christian Publishing Services, Inc., 1987), p. 52. Available from Randy Shankle Ministries, P. O. Box 8320, Marshall, Texas 75671.
3. *Oxford American Dictionary,* p. 40.
4. "Lexical Aids to the New Testament," *The Hebrew-Greek Key Study Bible,* pp. 1689, 1690.

PART II
Workbook for Sanctification/Deliverance

10
The Path to Freedom

The Spirit of the Lord God is upon me;
because the Lord hath anointed me
to preach good tidings unto the meek (teachable)
he hath sent me to bind up the brokenhearted,
to proclaim liberty to the captives,
and the opening of the prison to them that are bound;
To proclaim the acceptable year of the Lord,
the day of vengeance of our God;
to comfort all that mourn;
to appoint unto them that mourn in Zion,
to give unto them beauty for ashes,
the oil of joy for mourning,
the garment of praise for the spirit of heaviness;
that they might be called trees of righteousness,
the planting of the Lord, that he might be glorified.
Isaiah 61:1-3

—

Jesus was sent not simply to provide salvation—atonement for the sins of the world—but to provide healing for those who are physically or emotionally hurt or sick, and to provide freedom from the bondage of satanic snares and curses. When He returned to Heaven to sit at His Father's right hand (Rom. 8:34), He delegated the responsibility of carrying out these things to His Body, the Church.

> **And all things are of God, who hath reconciled us to himself by Jesus Christ, and hath given to us the ministry of reconciliation.**
> **Now then we are ambassadors for Christ, as though God did beseech you by us: we pray you in Christ's stead, be ye reconciled to God.**
> **2 Corinthians 5:18,20**

As we have discussed in earlier chapters, when a person is born again, his spirit is quickened and made alive to God. In other words, he gets a new spirit as a gift from God for none of us is responsible for the "dead" spirit with which he is born. However, the soul must still be renewed to the image of Christ in order to be in tune or under authority to the new spirit—which is under the authority of the Holy Spirit. Because the will, or free choice, was involved in the formation of the present soul, the renewal of that soul must be done by the Holy Spirit in cooperation with the will. We are responsible for our souls. The Holy Spirit will renew us from sin-conscious minds to God-conscious minds as we decide to exchange one "program" (a set of behavior patterns) or one set of emotions for a principles or behavior in tune with the mind and the character of Jesus.

There may be obstacles to overcome first, however: demonic influence or oppression, inner vows and bitter-root judgments, and wounds of the spirit. Any of these hindrances can cause a person to be double-minded (James 1:6-8), to think one way and act another, to want to change and yet not

The Path to Freedom

be able. How can you overcome these? The answer to that question is "through the ministry of sanctification."

Steps Along the Path to Freedom

1. Become a new creature (2 Cor. 5:17) in Christ, be born again—John 3:3-7, 16; 1 John 5:1-4, Romans 10:8-11, John 6:37.

> **That if thou shalt confess with thy mouth Jesus as Lord, and shalt believe in thine heart that God hath raised him from the dead, thou *shalt* be saved.**
> **Romans 10:9**

2. Confess as sin any carnal sins as opposed to other sins, any rebellion against authority, any involvement in the occult and any unforgiveness against others or against yourself:

   Confession of sins—1 John 1:9.

   Rebellion—1 Samuel 15:23. Dishonoring parents (no matter what they did to you) can bring a curse, as we have mentioned previously. Ephesians 6:2 says that honoring your father and mother is *the first commandment with blessing*. Submitting to constituted authority (when it does not conflict with the Word of God) can be as simple as obeying traffic laws or complying with the rules in a grocery store, rules set up by the "authority" (the management) of that store.

   Occult Involvement (amounts to idolatry)—Exodus 20:3-6; Deuteronomy 18:10-13; Acts 19:18,19.

   Unforgiveness—Matthew 6:12-15, Luke 6:37, Ephesians 4:32, John 20:23. If past sins or mistakes keep coming up in your mind, you may not have forgiven yourself. (1 John 1:9, 2:1; Romans 8:34.) In that case, you are actually exalting yourself. You are saying, "*My* sins are so great that even the blood of Jesus cannot cover them!" If the memories continue to torment you, you may be under the oppression of an harrassing or a "memory-recall" spirit. In which case, you need to find a good sanctification ministry. Unforgiveness creates ungodly soul ties between you and those whom you will not forgive and between you and the things in yourself that you will not forgive.

3. Break ungodly soul ties (emotional or mental ties that are perverted, ungodly, or negative)—Matthew 16:19. Canadian pastor-author Alexander Ness gives the following example:

    > Case 9: This concerns a young man, a Christian, who was never able to leave his mother and cling only to his wife. The mother was a Christian and a very good woman, but she was in control of the husband and son. After taking authority over an umbilical soul-tie, the son was freed for the couple to be one, spirit, soul, and body.[1]

4. Break down strongholds—2 Corinthians 10:4. Ask God to heal the wounds in your spirit or your emotions. After you have forgiven everyone against whom you are holding something, those bitter roots (Heb. 12:15) will come out of you, and any wounds or scars that were caused by those events can be healed by the Holy Spirit. You will remember the same thing, but the hurt or anger or other negative emotion will be gone. Your reaction, the emotion with which you handled whatever happened (resentment, rebellion, unforgiveness, and so forth), made that incident into a stronghold and often has allowed a demon to "legally" oppress you.
5. Get deliverance—Mat. 12:33,34; Eph. 4:27, 6:11; 1 Timothy 3:6,7; 2 Timothy 2:26.
6. Be filled with the Holy Spirit—John 14:16,17; Acts 1:8, 2:4. You receive the Holy Spirit in the same way that you receive Jesus: by faith and by believing the Word of God.

The Path to Freedom

7. Commit to God. Set your will to be dead to sin and selfish ways (self) and alive to God and righteouness. Make Christ the center of your life, and look to Him to meet your needs—Galatians 2:20, Romans 6, Philippians 4:19.
8. Recognize God's work in your life—Psalm 18:32,33, 138:8; Ephesians 2:10; Galatians 5:22,23; Romans 5:3-5, 8:28,29; Philippians 1:6; 1 Thessalonians 5:24.
9. Learn who you are in Christ, and do not compare yourself with other people—Psalm 139:14,16,17; Proverbs 23:7; 2 Corinthians 10:5,12,17; Colossians 2:7.
10. Do not let other people put condemnation on you—Psalm 103:2, Romans 8:1,33,34; 2 Corinthians 10:5; Ephesians 6:11-18; 1 John 1:9, 3:19-21. If others reject you, and you have done nothing wrong, view that rejection as their problem. Stand against condemnation in your own thought life, and cast it down. The Bible says there is no condemnation for those who love and serve Him. (Rom. 8:1.)
11. Control what you put into your mind, and what you think about. This will produce Godly thoughts and behavior—Psalm 119:1-11; Proverbs 16:3; Philippians 4:6-9; Colossians 3:2,16; 2 Timothy 1:7; 1 Peter 1:13; 1 John 4:18.
12. Help other people. Reach out to minister to others in need. When you "sow" love and help into the lives of others, you will reap it again in your own life when you need it—Romans 5:5; Ephesians 5:2; 1 Thessalonians 3:12; 1 John 4:10,11,19.

These steps will bring about sanctification of the soul. Remember we discussed earlier that sanctification is past, present, and future? Your spirit is sanctified when you are born again, and your body at the resurrection. Soul sanctification is a process.

Steps 2-5 should be undertaken through your pastor or through deliverance and counseling ministries called of

God. These steps involve the binding of principalities and powers, and this requires members of the Body operating in unity.

Binding Principalities and Powers

Christians have been given a "power of attorney" from Jesus, the authority to heal the sick and cast out demons, as well as to tell the world the good news about Him. (Mark 16:15-18.) However, in dealing with satanic rulers, it is well to remember Jude's words concerning those who **speak evil of dignities** (Jude 8).

> **Yet Michael the archangel, when contending with the devil he disputed about the body of Moses, durst not bring against him a railing accusation, but said, The Lord rebuke thee.**
>
> **Jude 9**

Travis Walters says in *He Laughs in the Heavens:*

> I close with this warning: if your fellowship fails to qualify in any of . . . three areas, *it is extremely dangerous for you to engage in the type of warfare which has been described* . . .! By all means set your spiritual house in order first, or you will find yourself captured by the very forces which you are seeking to bind.[2]

Walters says a fellowship of believers can bind strong men if they have holiness (Ps. 15:1,2), submission, and commitment. In other words, sin hinders and, in many cases, stops believers' authority from operating. Rebels cannot bind the forces of rebellion, and without commitment to God and to each other in the Body, there cannot be the unity necessary to come together in agreement. The Word says one can put a thousand to flight, but two can put ten thousand (Deut.

The Path to Freedom

32:30), but if the two are not walking and talking together in agreement, they can put nothing to flight. Walters continues:

> So there are these three things: holiness, submission, commitment. I realize that among different groups there are variations of interpretation concerning these essentials, and that is all right provided the *spirit* of each ingredient is present. (God is not impressed with legalistic holiness, submission, or commitment.)
>
> In Matthew 18, Jesus stated:
>
> **Again I say to you, That if two of you shall agree on earth as touching any thing that they shall ask, it shall be done for them of my Father which is in heaven. For where two or three are gathered together in my name, there am I in the midst of them.** (vs. 19,20).
>
> The word *agree* is the same word from which we get "symphony." Jesus is saying if two "symphonize," i.e., flow in perfect spiritual harmony in prayer, what they request will be done. Unquestionably, the approach to this harmony consists of the three essentials which I have outlined here. Without them, there can be no true unity.[2a]

Once a ministry or group who feels called into deliverance or sanctification has met the scriptural requirements listed above—along with any other things brought to their awareness by the Holy Spirit, then wait for Him to open the doors. *Do not push on doors* or try to initiate your own ministry. Anything built by the flesh is of the flesh. Your "gift" or calling will make a way for you. Make yourself ready and available, and God will make the opportunity. He will bring people to you or give you a "witness" that someone needs help, or He will have your pastor tell you when you are ready.

Remember, when you move into the same sort of sessions we are discussing in this book, you are *not* counseling in the sense of the world's (or even religious) counseling and you are *not* there for the purpose of hearing confessions. You are there to allow the Holy Spirit to do His work through your mouth and your hands. You are there to exercise the authority of Jesus as His representative.

A Word of Caution: Use wisdom and great judgment in deciding what to tell, or how much, of all the things the Holy Spirit will show or tell you during these sessions. *It is not necessary to tell everything you see or know,* only what they need to know.

End Notes

1. Alexander William Ness, *Transference of Spirits* (Canada: Ontario. Copyright (c) 1984 by Agapre Publications Inc., P. O. Box 2068, Stn. C, Downsview, Ontario, Canada M3N 2S8), p. 12.
2, 2a. Travis Walters, *He Who Laughs in the Heavens* (California: San Jose, Fellowship Ministries, P. O. Box 32752, San Jose, CA 95152. Copyright (c) 1978 by Travis Walters), pp. 98,100.

11

Prayer of Sanctification: Sequence and Procedure

The Holy Spirit is the Sanctifier. *You are not the Sanctifier.* Let the Holy Spirit work through you. Also, counselors must be cleansed people set aside for holiness, working together in complete unity, and under the covering of a church. Each session should be under the spiritual authority of a pastor or of a male counselor. Do not move into the deliverance ministry prematurely or rapidly, or you may get hit with some type of sickness or with other problems. However, such attacks can be warded off with praises lifted to God.

Use the name of Jesus often!

I remember some years ago hearing Oral Roberts tell of Jesus appearing to him as he lay in a hospital bed and saying, "Use My name much." The Lord already had spoken this to me: "I want you to learn to use My name." About that time Kenneth Hagin's book, *The Name of Jesus,* was published.[1] It is a really good book on this subject. The Bible says the name of

Jesus is above every other name, that every name will bow the knee to that name. (Eph. 1:21, Philip. 2:10.)

Prayer Preceding a Session: Heavenly Father, You said in Your Word, "Not by might, nor by power, but by My spirit." (Zech. 4:6.) So we ask You, Holy Spirit, to do the ministering. Lord, You said, "The Yoke shall be destroyed because of the anointing." (Is. 10:27.) So we thank you in advance for the anointing of the Holy Spirit in this session.

1. Ask, "Why do you wish sanctification?"
   It is important to know if the person wants help or if someone else (parent or spouse) has forced them to come. The individual must want it, or the sanctification process will not work any more than the salvation process.
2. Start the session with everyone praying in the Spirit.
3. Explain to the counselee how to receive:
   a. Keep your mind on Jesus.
   b. Do not pray, simply set yourself in agreement with the counselors.
   c. Relax!
   d. Do not analyze or try to reason out what is happening.
   e. Be a receiver.
4. Next pray for the following:
   a. Total victory for the counselee.
   b. Unity between each counselor, the counselee, and the Holy Spirit.
   c. Pray for the gifts of the Holy Spirit to operate and flow as the Holy Spirit desires: 1) tongues, 2) interpretation, 3) prophecy, 4) faith, 5) gifts of healings, 6) working of miracles, 7) discerning of spirits, 8) word of wisdom, 9) word of knowledge.
   d. Pray for protection, putting on the whole armor of God:

Prayer of Sanctification: Sequence and Procedure

a) helmet of salvation, b) breastplate of righteousness, c) gird up the loins with truth, d) shoe your feet with the preparation of the Gospel of Peace, e) above all, to be covered with the shield of faith, and f) to go forth with the Sword of the Spirit which is the Word of God. (Eph. 6:11.)

Prayer of Protection: Heavenly Father, I come to you in the name of Jesus. I now take authority over the principalities, powers, rulers of darkness, wicked spirits in high places. (Eph. 6:12.) I bind them up in the name of Jesus. I specifically name the Jezebel, Antichrist, and Death and Hades principalities, and bind them up also. Heavenly Father, I loose warring angels to do whatever warfare or ministry is necessary to protect me, my family, and each of these people that we are praying for today as well as all that you have made each of us stewards over.

5. Next, speak out specifically the commands you have for any demonic forces that might be involved. (You *pray* to God and *speak* to satanic entities.)

Now, by the blood of Jesus Christ, I take authority over spirits of confrontation, distraction, deception, confusion, repression, competition, guilt, shame, embarrassment, fear, and over the strong man of rejection, the strong man of rebellion, the strong man of soul power, and over all demonic power seated in the soul. I bind these up *in the Name of Jesus*, I command them to loose their hold, leave, come out, come off of them, and I cast you away from all we have been made stewards and heirs of. I bind all evil spirits. I curse any roots by which these evil spirits operate in this person and command those roots to die. I break their power over this person and command the evil spirits involved here to be cast away from all we have been made stewards and heirs of *in the*

Name of Jesus and through His authority purchased for me by His blood—by the blood of the Lord Jesus Christ, by the blood of the Lord Jesus Christ, by the blood of the Lord Jesus Christ, by the blood of the Lord Jesus Christ. So be it.

6. Proceed as follows, with *no one* exempted.
   a. Have the counselee confess the sinner's prayer according to Romans 10:9,10. Be alert to a witness from the Holy Spirit as to whether the counselee really has accepted Jesus in his heart or whether he has simply assented mentally.

   Sinner's Prayer: Heavenly Father, "I confess with my mouth the Lord Jesus and believe in my heart that God has raised Him from the dead. For You said with the heart one believes to righteousness, and with the mouth confession is made to salvation. Heavenly Father, I said it with my mouth, and I believe it in my heart. So be it."
   b. Ask, "Are you filled with the Holy Spirit?" If not, make a note to have them ask for the infilling at the end of the session after sanctification.
7. Go through the rejection/rebellion, sanctification, principalities, and health problems work sheet.[2] Go through each item and have the counselee make the following statements:
   a. I confess each involvement with _____ as sin. (James 5:16.)
   b. I renounce each involvement *in the Name of Jesus*. (2 Cor. 4:2.)
   c. I ask for forgiveness from my Heavenly Father *in the Name of Jesus*. (1 John 1:9.)
   d. I accept forgiveness *in Jesus' name*. (1 John 3:20.)
8. Pray for people not present. (John 20:23.)

   When using the sanctification worksheet for yourself and others, always pray for yourself and your helper at

Prayer of Sanctification: Sequence and Procedure

least once a day when ministering to others. When praying for sanctification for others include their marriages, family problems, problems with friends or employees/employer, and so forth, pray for those not at the session who are involved in the situation. Name each person you wish to help. Then write their names down on both sides of the work sheet. This will make it easier to remember their names.

9. Now pray over each item on the work sheet individually.

    By the blood of the Lord Jesus Christ, I take authority over the spirit of _____ that has been assigned to or is operating through (name of person). I bind you up and curse your roots and command them to dry up and die, by the blood of the Lord Jesus Christ. I command you to loose your hold and be cast into the sea, by the blood of the Lord Jesus Christ. I cut this person free from you by the Sword of the Holy Spirit, which is the Word of God. I loose you from your assignment.

    Command the evil spirit to go *by the blood of the Lord Jesus Christ* several times, at least seven. If evil spirits do not yield right away, spend a little more time in prayer to find out the exact problem.

    Now, in the closing prayer, do this:

10. Cut the counselee loose from the cords of the principalities with the Sword of the Spirit, which is the Word of God. (Heb. 4:12, Mat. 18:19.)
11. Cut the ancestral bloodline as well as all curses, hexes, and sins that have been transmitted from forefathers.
12. Pray for healing of all hurts, wounds, broken hearts, and traumas, and for the healing of memories.
13. Take authority over every negative word, prayer, and statement that has been spoken or prayed that was out of the will of God from conception to present. Pray, "I bind them up in the name of Jesus and command them to be cast into the sea." (Mark 11:23.)

14. Having ministered to everything, pray that the counselee will be filled with the fruit of the Spirit (Gal. 5:22,23.):

    a) love, b) joy, c) peace, d) longsuffering, e) gentleness, f) goodness, g) faith, h) meekness, and i) temperance j) confidence and boldness.
15. Now pray for the Baptism of the Holy Spirit if they have not received it.
16. Next, pray for the Holy Spirit to minister His gifts to the counselee *as He wills*. His gifts are the weapons of our warfare (1 Cor. 12, 2 Cor. 10:4):

    a) tongues, b) interpretation, c) prophecy, d) faith, e) gifts of healings, f) working of miracles, g) discerning of spirits, h) word of wisdom, and i) word of knowledge.
17. Pray for the operations of God (a motivational or "Fatherly characteristic" given by God to each child of His) to begin operating in the life of the counselee[3] (Rom. 12:6b-8):

    a) giving, b) administration, c) mercy, d) exhortation, e) teaching, f) serving, or g) prophecy.
18. Next pray for this person to put on the whole armor of God (Eph. 6:11), and tell them to do this daily:

    a) helmet of salvation, b) breastplate of righteousness, c) gird up the loins with truth, d) shoe your feet with the preparation of the Gospel of peace, e) above all, to be covered with the shield of faith, and f) to go forth with the Sword of the Spirit, the Word of God.
19. Always pray over each person that they will be bold in using the Word of God.
20. Loose the angel assigned to each person present, as well those assigned to minister for (Heb. 1:14) each person for whom you are praying, to go forth *in the Name of Jesus* to prepare the way for each person's ministry, work and business.

Prayer of Sanctification: Sequence and Procedure

21. Pray for each person to prosper spiritually, physically, financially, materially, mentally, and in all other areas of life so the Word of God may be established in the earth. (See Ephesians, chapters 1 and 3.)
22. Pray for each person to have favor with all men, especially with those who can help them grow and develop in the Body of Christ. Then pray for all those who have anything against your counselee as well as yourself. Forgive them, and pray for each of them.
23. Pray and close all occult and cultic doors that may have been opened intentionally or inadvertently. I cover each person by name with the blood of the Lord Jesus Christ over their lives. I do this several times. There must be a blood-covering protection over each person at this point with no exception. Also, there must be protection prayed over everything over which each of us has been made stewards and heirs.

End Notes

1. Kenneth Hagin, *The Name of Jesus*, Kenneth Hagin Ministries, P. O. Box 50126, Tulsa, OK 74150.
2. For those who are in the ministry or already operating in the areas of deliverance or counseling, Appendix A contains our work sheets.
3. Marilyn Hickey, *Motivational Gifts* (Texas: Dallas. Copyright (c) 1983) by Word of Faith Publishing, P. O. Box 819000, Dallas, Texas 75381).

12
Standing in the Gap

> And I sought for a man among them,
> that should make up the hedge,
> and stand in the gap before me for the land,
> that I should not destroy it:
> but I found none.
>
> Ezekiel 22:30

By "building a hedge" through prayer and the authority of Jesus around loved ones, saved or unsaved, or around an unfaithful partner, Satan is not able any longer to take them captive at his will. God has a claim on them in love and will begin to turn what Satan meant for evil for good. (2 Tim. 2:24,25,26; Gen. 50:20.)

A certain man whose mother had come to us for counseling discovered that his wife was secretly seeing one of his employees. He learned about the "hedge/covering of protection" that he could claim in prayer for his wife, and he used it.

It was not long until the affair had been broken off, his wife had repented, and their home was restored.

A wife learned that her husband was spending time with an older woman. She learned further that he was planning to leave her and marry this older woman. She was told how to pray for a "hedge/covering of protection" around her husband. The next evening he received a phone call from the other woman telling him that she wanted to break off their relationship.

These are only a few of the many illustrations which Christians are experiencing as a result of building a hedge around their loved ones. However, there is far more to the story than just praying a certain prayer. This is not a "formula" or a ritual. The scriptural basis for the hedge is found in several places.

First of all, God looks for an intercessor to make up a hedge of protection or to stand in the gap for individuals as well as nations. (Eze. 22:30.) Job is an example of such a man in the Old Testament. (Job 1:5-10.)

Job feared that his sons and daughters might sin and offend God, so he interceded for them. He was a perfect and upright man, and God **made an hedge about him, and about his house, and about all that he hath on every side** (Job 1:10). Job had a blood covenant through animal sacrifices. (Job 1:5.) With this hedge or covering, Satan was not able to take anyone in Job's family captive at his will. But Job got into fear, making a hole in his hedge, and Satan did attack him.

> **For the thing which I greatly feared has come upon me, and that which I was afraid of is come unto me.**
>
> **Job 3:25**

A better illustration of the hedge/covering is found in Hosea. God promised to make a "hedge of thorns" around Hosea's adulterous wife (symbolic of Israel) so that her lovers would lose interest in her. After God built a hedge/covering of thorns around Hosea's wife, and her lovers left her, she decided to return to her husband.

The New Testament counterpart to this truth is illustrated in Christ's intercession for Peter and for the other disciples. It is also illustrated in Paul's prayer for those under his spiritual care (Eph. 1:15-23). The blood covenant of Christians was not made with the blood of animals but with the blood of the Lord Jesus Christ.

> **Neither by the blood of goats and calves, but by his own blood he entered in once into the holy place, having obtained eternal redemption for us.**
> **Hebrews 9:12**

The basic reason for the hedge is found in 2 Corinthians 10:4:

> **For the weapons of our warfare are not carnal, but mighty through God to the pulling down of strong holds.**

This emphasizes the fact that Satan is able to have powerful holds on our souls—minds, wills, and emotions—but that through God we can and must pull them down. The purpose of "binding Satan" (Mark 3:27) and building a hedge/covering around someone is so that you can proceed to the **casting down of imaginations, and every high thing that exalteth itself against the knowledge of God, and bringing into captivity every thought to the obedience of Christ** (2 Cor. 10:5).

However, Hosea found that if his wife was to remain under his authority and protection, there were several things that he had to do. These are listed in Hosea 2:14-16. We are aware of a number of cases in which a husband or wife built a hedge around an unfaithful partner through prayer, saw the return of that partner, and then failed to follow up on the victory. Soon Satan regained a foothold in that partner's life. Thus, the following steps are very essential.

Steps to Establishing and Maintaining a Hedge

1. Be certain that *you* are really born again.

   If you are in doubt, read the prayers for salvation and the Scriptures in Chapter 8. We become a child of God only through putting our full faith and trust for salvation in the finished work of the Lord Jesus Christ, in His dying for us and being raised from the dead:

   Not by works of righteousness which we have done, but according to his mercy he saved us... (Titus 3:5).

2. Cleanse yourself of all sin.

   God delighted in building a hedge/covering of protection around Job and all his family and possessions, because Job was a perfect and upright man. He feared God and hated evil. We can claim the righteousness of Christ by confessing our sins and cleansing our mind, life, and home of anything that grieves the Spirit of God and hinders His work in our lives. **Make not provision for the flesh, to fulfill the lust thereof** (Romans 13:14). If you have not been through sanctification, you need to do that before you proceed in this prayer.

3. Build a "hedge/covering of protection" through prayer.

   The following prayer is an example of building a "hedge/covering of protection" around an unfaithful marriage partner.

   Heavenly Father, I ask You *by the blood of the Lord Jesus Christ*, to build a covering through the blood of the Lord Jesus Christ and a hedge of protection around my partner. I pray that through this covering any other lover will lose interest and depart. I base this prayer on Your Word which commands that what You have joined together, let not man put asunder. (Mat. 19:6.)

Standing in the Gap

4. Restore the oneness in your relationship, and bring the two of you into a renewed unity. (Hos. 2:13-16.)
5. Cast down wrong reasonings.

In the spirit of friendship and fellowship, cast down false reasonings in the mind of your partner by wisely using God's Word. Bring every thought of your own into captivity to the obedience of Christ. Also pray for healing of memories, healing of wounded spirits, healing of a broken heart.

What happens when you put a "covering of protection" around an unfaithful partner?

That partner will lose momentum in the wrong direction in which he or she is headed, any other lovers will leave, the resulting troubles will create a desire to return to the home or the mate.

A covering will be ineffective if you have not resolved all past offenses, or if you do not follow through with scriptural steps of action. The prayer for a spiritual hedge includes three prerequisites:

1. Your spiritual credentials must be in order. We are able to approach a holy God through the righteousness of Jesus. Christ's death and resurrection defeated Satan's power.

> **But thanks be to God, which giveth us the victory through our Lord Jesus Christ.**
> **1 Corinthians 15:57**

On the basis of this, we pray in the Name of Jesus and by the blood of the Lord Jesus Christ.

2. Your request must be specific. The more precise we are in prayer, the easier it is to judge the scriptural basis on which we are standing, and the more alert we will be in seeing His answer to it. To paraphrase James 4:2: **Ye have not because ye ask not exactly what you desire.**
3. You must understand your scriptural authority. Every request must be based on the will of God as revealed in His

Word, the sword of the Spirit. (Eph 6:17.) We are able to overcome Satan **by the blood of the Lamb and by the word of** (our) **testimony....** (Rev. 12:11.)

How to Win a Wayward Person

Scripture references:
Ezekiel 22:30; Job 1:5-10; Hosea 2:5-7, 14-16; Luke 22:31-32; John 17, 2 Corinthians 11:28; Mark 3:27; Titus 3:5; Romans 5:8, 10:9, 13:14; Matthew 19:6, and 1 Corinthians 10:4,5.

Appendix
Sanctification Worksheet

[Follow procedure outlined in Chapter 11.]

___ REJECTION:*

- ___ Accusation toward others
- ___ Despair
- ___ Persecution
- ___ Distrust*
- ___ Suspicion
- ___ Jealousy*
- ___ Envy
- ___ Fears
- ___ Nervousness
- ___ Tension
- ___ Talkativeness
- ___ Sensitiveness
- ___ Loneliness
- ___ Timidity
- ___ Shyness
- ___ Self-awareness
- ___ Pouting
- ___ Vivid Imagination
- ___ Unreality
- ___ Daydreaming
- ___ Fantasy
- ___ Withdrawal
- ___ Unfairness
- ___ Vanity
- ___ Pride
- ___ Perfection
- ___ Condemnation/Guilt
- ___ Self-pity
- ___ Suicide
- ___ Hopelessness
- ___ Despondency
- ___ Depression
- ___ False Responsibility
- ___ False Compassion
- ___ Fear of Judgment
- ___ Compulsive Confession
- ___ Self-accusation
- ___ Sex Perversion
- ___ Fantasy Lust
- ___ Lust
- ___ Fear of Rejection*
- ___ Self-rejection*

__ REBELLION:*
__ BITTERNESS:*

- __ Self-righteousness
- __ Criticism
- __ Unbelief
- __ Doubt
- __ Insanity
- __ Unworthiness
- __ Insecurity
- __ Anxiety
- __ Projection
- __ Worry
- __ Confrontation
- __ Paranoia
- __ Hurricane
- __ Judgmentalism
- __ Unteachableness
- __ Selfishness
- __ Stubborness*
- __ Terror
- __ Battering
- __ Stupor
- __ Escape
- __ Division

- __ Frustration*
- __ Retaliation
- __ Impatience
- __ Intolerance
- __ Anger
- __ Murder
- __ Memory Recall
- __ Unforgiveness
- __ Violence
- __ Resentment*
- __ Hatred*
- __ Possessiveness
- __ Control
- __ Strife
- __ Gossip
- __ Lying
- __ Lack of Identity*
- __ Assault
- __ Deceit
- __ Confusion
- __ Legion
- __ Old Man

*Starred spirits usually affect adopted children or those from broken homes.

Sanctification Worksheet

Primary Evil Spirits Under the Three Main Principalities

__ JEZEBEL PRINCIPALITY*

- __ OCCULT SPIRIT*
- __ Cult spirit
- __ Jezebel spirit
- __ Religious spirit
- __ Unclean spirit
- __ Independent spirit
- __ Home-wrecking spirit
- __ Bloodline Cult Ties spirit
- __ Idol Worship spirit

- __ Control spirit
- __ Shell spirit
- __ Ahab spirit
- __ Moab spirit (incest)
- __ Queen Mother spirit
- __ Baby Terror spirit
- __ Church-wrecking spirit
- __ Witchcraft spirit
- __ Madonna spirit

__ ANTICHRIST PRINCIPALITY*

- __ Top dog spirit
- __ False doctrine
- __ False teaching
- __ Spiritual deafness
- __ Spiritual blindness
- __ Spiritual ignorance
- __ Humanism

- __ Deception
- __ Seduction
- __ Delusion
- __ Self-preservation
- __ Self-love
- __ TRADITION*
- __ Inheritance

__ DEATH AND HADES PRINCIPALITY*

- __ INFIRMITIES*
- __ Suicide
- __ Self-destruction
- __ Fear
- __ Disease
- __ Tiredness
- __ Famines
- __ Plagues
- __ Alcoholism
- __ Nicotine
- __ Drugs

- __ Death
- __ Destruction
- __ Sickness
- __ Affliction
- __ Fatigue
- __ Weakness
- __ Poverty
- __ Fear of Failure
- __ Worry
- __ Confusion
- __ Darkness

* All spirits that are capitalized should be the last ones to be cast out.

Spirits of infirmity or death spirits operate under the principality above. In addition to casting out the spirit, the counselor needs to then command the gland or the organ or the limb or whatever body system is involved to operate properly. Speak healing to the body areas involved. Some of these spirits may be operating through generation inheritances. In which case, those ties and curses must be broken before the spirit will come out or before healing will take place. In any of these lists, if any spirits are difficult to cast out, put a star by them and come back to them later. Usually, they will be easier to dislodge after their support-demons have been cast out. In all of these lists, *please remember to be led by the Holy Spirit*. He is in charge. These are not "formulas" or "rituals," but guidelines in order not to inadvertently overlook something.

Infirmity Spirits and/or Death Spirits:

Listed below are some of these kinds of spirits with which we have dealt. All of these operate under the authority of the Death and Hades Principality. There are many others, of course. I have come to believe that all sicknesses and diseases involve an evil spirit. Therefore, you can add to this list as you find other things:

Appendicitis, back problems, emphysema, fevers, cancer, thyroid problems (goiter), headaches, diabetes, heart attacks or disease, heart enlargement and other heart problems, hardened blood veins, arteries, or blood system, cholesterol, high or low blood pressure, cysts, infections, all itching, kidney infections or stones, leukemia, female problems or disorders, all kinds of nausea, all kinds of infections, physical weaknesses, fatigue, liver problems or diseases, all kinds of allergies, respiratory diseases, skin diseases or con-

Sanctification Worksheet

ditions, disorders of the digestive system (worry), bone marrow, metabolism, bladder problems, and ear, nose, and eye problems.

Again let me say, *it is necessary to be sensitive to the Holy Spirit* to properly speak the healing required. After a spirit of epilepsy, you should command the nervous system to be healed and restored or command a new system. With the adrenal gland, the spirits involved are usually unforgiveness or worry (stress). With Alzheimer's, it becomes necessary to speak healing or creative re-growth to the brain. With a slipped disc, you must also command all inflammation to leave. We highly recommend Charles and Frances Hunter's videos and seminars on deliverance and healing.

Common Symbols of Evil Spirits

Many times during sanctification sessions, the Holy Spirit will show a evil spirit to the person operating in discernment in a symbolic form rather than in its literal form. Perhaps it is because actual sight of evil spirits would be too demoralizing to the person, or perhaps the person does not actually operate in "discernment of spirits" but the symbols shown them are a form of "word of knowledge." More than likely, it is because if the "see-er" saw the actual evil spirit, he or she still would not know what to call out of the person. John Sandford calls these symbolic pictures "God's cartoons."[1] Sometimes the Holy Spirit will give a name or the name of a category, such as "envy," "pride," and so forth. Why He chooses to give revelation in various ways is His business!

Apparently this form of communication is the third of the five ways in which Deity speaks to man that are listed in Numbers 12:6-8: dreams, visions, "dark speech" (KJV) or "riddles" (NIV), still small voice, and directly or "face to face."[2] At any rate, a number of books on deliverance and the experiences of our own and related ministries show similarities in these depictions of certain evil spirits.

You should remember, however, that the Holy Spirit *always* is the final authority, not your own mind. At times, walls mean a shell spirit assigned by a jezebelic principality. Other times, the sight of a wall may simply mean the person needs emotional healing. A green lizard or alligator or snake most often is some form of jealousy, but once recently, a evil spirit shown as a tiny green lizard was a form of fear—fear of not being believed. Therefore, rather than memorizing symbols, check each symbol with the Holy Spirit for the interpretation. In other words, *He will not only show you symbols or riddles but interpret them for you.*

Alzheimer's disease: Appears sometimes as mushrooms.
Antichrist-related spirit: Appears sometimes as a "thunderbird," a messenger of Satan. Same thing as a "morning bird" of American Indian lore, or as a swine (pig).
Anger: A wolf lying low.
Attack (accusing) spirit: A bulldog.
Confusion spirit: Usually looks like a rat on each shoulder of a person speaking different things into each ear.
Control spirit: This spirit may be shown as a spider, an octopus, or a crab. It controls through its arms leading to many hurts and wounds in a person. When the person seems to be getting freedom, it will pull one of its tentacles to cause the person to draw back. It says, "No one sees me," and will slowly bring bitterness, hatred, unforgivness, and suicide to the surface. Others have seen this as many demons around a table, a corporate operation.
Death spirit: Skulls, hooded figures, sometimes as owls or coffins.
Drug or alcohol spirit: Sometimes in the form of a snake.

Sanctification Worksheet

Emotional spirit: Hurricanes or tornadoes.

Familiar spirit: Many times this will be a spirit the same shape and size as the person but with no face or with oriental features. Other times, it may be seen as an imp (what used to be called "Brownies" in fairy and folk tales) sitting on the shoulder or head.

Fear spirit: Also appears as a snake attacking or wrapping around a person from head to foot.

Generation inheritance spirit: Many-layered cakes.

Idol worship spirit: Can be anything placed before God—money, one's spouse or children, a country. Also, this can be a generation spirit. Images can show as the thing itself, religious statues, totem poles. In one case of a food-addiction evil spirit, it appeared as a sugar bowl.

Jezebel spirit: Almost always in the form of a ape or gorilla; although in at lease one instance, the evil spirit appeared with a grotesque face of a woman—a woman with exaggerated make-up, a crown, and long, sharp fingernails.

Judgmental spirit: As an elephant. *Memory recall spirits also* may appear as an elephant.

Legion: Appears as a swarm of fleas, flies, or hornets.

Lust spirit: Almost always in the form of a frog.

Madonna spirit: Usually in the form of the stereotyped madonna. Causes a woman to be domineering, dogmatic, and work to have everything her own way.

Occult spirit: Appears as colors, or sometimes in a manifestation of the person's eyeballs spinning around and around. Also may be seen as an astrological sign.

Panic: (A form of fear) Lots of little "things" (or mice) scurrying around.

Passive spirit: A blanket, or a person hiding under a bed.

Poverty spirit: A raggedy man or woman.

Pride spirit: A rooster or a frog with chests all puffed out, strutting around. The person may be shown dressed as a princess or a prince.

Queen Mother spirit: A queen bee.

Religious spirit: Overlaps with idol worship. We have seen it as an old-fashioned one-horse plow, as the little cap worn by some religions, or as a prim lady-school-teacher type of the last century with hair pulled back in a bun, extremely neat, and high-buttoned shoes with a long black dress.

Shell spirit: Any kind of false protection. May appear as a wall, shell, bottle, turtle, transparent garbage bag, etc.

Spiritual blindness and deafness spirits—often over churches: Appear as monkeys with hands over the eyes or ears, or as bands around the head.

Spiritual ignorance spirit: A hair net over the head.

Suicide spirit: Usually in the form of a black bird.

Tradition spirit: Often seen as a dragon.

Unforgiveness spirit: This also may appear as a snake wrapped around the person, or as chains or cords

Witchcraft spirit: Shown as a witch or as hex signs.

Worry spirit: Darkness or a whirlwind.

Note: Ken and Nancy Curtis' book, *Tormented*, has a very valuable center section "List of Common Evil Spirits." This does not give the appearances, but does list them under appropriate strong men who dispatch or assign them.[3]

Biblical Curses for Specific Disobediences

1. Any sin worthy of the death penalty under civil governments also is cursed by God. (Deut. 21:22,23.)
2. Cursing or mistreating God's children (Israelites, Jews, and today's children of promise made up of all earthly races). (Gen. 12:3 and 27:29, Num. 24:9.)
3. Being a willing deceiver. (Gen. 27:12, Josh. 9:23, Jer. 48:10, Mal. 1:14.)

Sanctification Worksheet

4. An adulterous woman (Num. 5:27), and adulterers. (Deut. 22:22-27, Job 24:15-18.)
5. Disobedience to specific commandments of the Lord. (Deut. 11:28, Jer. 11:3, Dan. 9:11.)
6. Idolatry. (Deut. 4:8,9 and 29:18,19, Ex. 20:5, Jer. 44:8.)
7. Keeping or owning cursed objects. (Deut. 7:25, Josh. 6:18, Acts 19:19.) This includes representations of unclean creatures such as owls and frogs, because they have been used in occult and idolatrous practices at least since Egypt was an empire and because apparently creatures such as these are easier to be demon-possessed. (Ex. 8, Lev. 11:17, Ps. 78:45 and 105:30, Rev. 16:13.)
8. The house of the wicked. (Prov. 3:33.)
9. Refusing to come to the Lord's help, or to the help of those who represent the Lord. (Judges 5:23.)
10. Not giving to the poor or not seeing the needs of the poor. (Prov. 28:27.)
11. The earth by reason of man's disobedience. (Isa. 24:3-6.)
12. If God's people who lived in Jerusalem rebelled, the city became a curse to all nations (Jer. 26:6)—which for hundreds of years it has been. Jerusalem has been a place where the sword (the curse of war) has fallen since the days of Jesus, and that curse is obviously still in effect. Before the time of Jesus, you can see in the Old Testament where Judah's rebellion brought the curse of war, famine, pestilence, drought and desolation, and even exile.
13. Stealing and swearing falsely by the Lord's name. (Zech. 5:4.)
14. Anyone who fails to give the glory for his ministry and works to God. (Mal. 2:2, Rev. 1:6.) His blessings are cursed.
15. Robbing God of tithes and offerings. (Mal. 3:9, Hag. 1:6-9.)
16. Men who put their wives above God. (Gen. 3:17.)
17. Lightly esteeming one's parents (Deut. 27:16), striking

one's parents (Ex. 21:15), cursing one's parents (Ex. 21:17), and rebelling against one's parents (Det. 21:18-21).
18. Making graven images. (Deut. 5:8 and 27:15, Ex. 20:4.)
19. Cheating people out of their property. (Deut. 27:17.)
20. Taking advantage of the blind (handicapped). (Deut. 27:18.)
21. Oppression of strangers, widows, or orphans. (Ex. 22:22-24, Deut. 27:19.)
22. Committing incest. (Deut. 27:20, 22.)
23. Children born of incestuous unions. (Gen. 19:36-38.)
24. Having sex with animals. (Ex. 22:19, Deut. 27:21.)
25. Secretly harming one's neighbors. (Deut. 27:24.)
26. Hired "contract men"—murderers of the innocent for pay (Deut. 27:25), and murderers in general. (Ex. 21:12.) Also indirect murder. (Ex. 21:14.)
27. On the other hand, there is a curse for *not* fighting in just causes. (Judges 5:23, 1 Kings 20:35-42, Jer. 48:10.) That can also mean being slack or indifferent to the ministry and the work of God, refusing to participate in the Great Commission.
28. The proud. (Ps. 119:21.)
29. Rewarding evil for good. (Prov. 17:13.)
30. Illegitimate children. (Deut. 23:2.)
31. Kidnapping. (Ex. 21:16, Deut. 24:7.)
32. Causing the unborn to die, or abortion. (Ex. 21:22,23.)
33. Not preventing death. (Ex. 21:29.)
34. Sacrificing to false gods. (Ex. 22:20.)
35. Blaspheming the Lord's name (Lev. 24:15,16), and swearing by His name falsely—misrepresenting Him (Zech. 5:3,4).
36. Attempting to turn anyone away from the Lord (Deut. 13:6-9, or hindering children from coming to the Lord (Matt. 19:14.)
37. Becoming involved in occultism (Deut. 5:9,10): following a horoscope (Deut. 17:12), involvement in witchcraft (Ex.

Sanctification Worksheet

22:18), participating in seances and fortune telling (Lev. 20:6), acting as a necromancer—a spiritualist—or a fortune teller (Lev. 20:27).
38. Rebellion against a pastor. (Deut. 17:12.)
39. Operating as a false prophet. (Deut. 18:19-22.)
40. Women who do not keep their virginity until marriage. (Deut. 22:13-21.) When one has sex outside of marriage, a curse is released into that life. It manifests as a cycle of marriage, divorce, and remarriage unless repentance comes and the curse is broken. Also, most of the time, deliverance will be necessary.
41. Not disciplining your children but putting them above God. (1 Sam. 2:17, 27-36.)
42. Cursing one's rulers or those in governmental authority. (Ex. 22:28, 1 Kings 2:8.9.)
43. Teaching rebellion against God. (Jer. 28:16,17.)
44. Refusing to warn those in sin. (Ez. 3:18-21.)
45. Defiling the Sabbath. (Ex. 31:14, Num. 15:32-36.)
46. Sacrificing human beings. (Lev. 20:2.)
47. Having intercourse during menstruation. (Lev. 20:18.)
48. Participating in perverse sex: homosexuality and lesbianism (Lev. 20:13), and sodomy, oral, and anal sex (Gen. 19:13, 24-25).
49. Hating someone. (Deut. 7:10.)
50. *And this one hits nearly every believer today:* being carnally minded. (Rom. 8:6.)
51. Deceitfulness. (Prov. 26:26.)
52. Not confirming and doing all the Word. (Deut. 27:26.)[4]

The curses can be manifested in different ways. Look up the scriptures listed and you will see that some of them have specific results mentioned. A curse on those in infidelity, for example, can manifest as bitterness (Prov. 5:3), poverty (Prov. 6:26), or destruction of the soul (Prov. 6:32). Proverbs 28:27 says hiding one's eyes from the poor will result in many a curse! As a matter of fact, the book of Proverbs spells out the consequences of many curses. Deception of neighbors can bring madness (Prov. 26:19), and a lack of understanding can bring great oppression (Prov. 28:16).

End Notes

1. John and Paula Sandford, *The Elijah Task* (New Jersey: Plainfield, Logos International, 1977).
2. Ibid. PP. 154,155.
3. Ken and Nancy Curtis, *Tormented* (Florida: Lakeland. Copyright 1984 by Spiritual Warfare Ministries, Inc., P. O. Box 6515, Lakeland, FL 33807), pp. 89-106.
4. Thanks go to Win Worley's books for some of these listings.

Bibliography

Barclay, Dr. Mark T. *Beware of Seducing Spirits* (Michigan: Midland. Mark Barclay Publications, P. O. Box 584, Midland, MI 48640. Copyright (c) 1987).
Basham, Don. *Can a Christian Have a Demon?* (Pennsylvania: Monroeville. Whitaker Books, 1971).
———*Deliver Us From Evil* (Copyright 1972 by author). (Virginia: Lincoln 22078. Chosen Books).
———*Jezebel Over America*, Cassette tape DT094 (Integrity Communications, P. O. Z, Mobile, AL 36616).
Bennett, Dennis and Rita. Christian Renewal Association, P. O. Box 576, Edmonds, WA 98020.
Curtis, Ken and Nancy. *Tormented* (Florida: Lakeland. Copyright 1984 by Spiritual Warfare Ministries, Inc., P. O. Box 6515, Lakeland, FL 33807), pp. 89-106.
Davis, Burnie. *How to Have God's Miracle Power in Your Life* (Oklahoma: Tulsa. Harrison House, Inc., 1982, 1986.)
Gasson, Raphael. *The Challenging Counterfeit* (Plainfield, New Jersey: Logos International, 1966.)

Gruen, Ernest. *Freedom to Choose* (19??) (Pennsylvania: Springdale. Whitaker House, Pittsburgh and Colfax Streets, Springdale, PA 15144.
——— *Touching the Heart of God* (1986, Whitaker House).
Hagin, Kenneth. *The Name of Jesus*, Kenneth Hagin Ministries, Broken Arrow, Oklahoma.
Hammond, Frank and Ida Mae. *Pigs in the Parlor* (1973)
——— *Kingdom Living for the Family* (1985) (Missouri: Kirkwood, Impact Books, 137 W. Jefferson, Kirkwood, MO 63122).
——— *Spiritual Warfare Series: Saints at War* (1986)
——— *Overcoming Rejection (1987)* (Texas: Plainview, The Children's Bread Ministry, P. O. Box 72, Plainview, TX 79073).
Hickey, Marilyn. *Motivational Gifts* (Texas: Dallas. Copyright (c) 1983) by Word of Faith Publishing, P. O. Box 819000, Dallas, Texas 75381).
Nee, Watchman. *Spiritual Authority* (New York: New York, Christian Fellowship Publishers Inc., 115115 Allecingie Parkway, Richmond, VA 23235. Copyright (c) 1972).
Ness, Alexander William. *Transference of Spirits* (Canada: Ontario. Copyright (c) 1984 by Agape Publications Inc., P. O. Box 2068, Stn. C, Downsview, Ontario, Canada M3N 2S8).
Park, Irene. *What Every Christian Should Know About Symbols, Signs, and Emblems*, Irene Park Ministries, P. O. Box 1394, New Port Richey, Florida 33552. Copyright (c) 1982.
Penn-Lewis, Jessie. *War on the Saints* (Pennsylvania: Fort Washington. The Christian Literature Crusade, Fort Washington, PA 19034, First American Edition . . . 1977).
Phillips, Phil. *Turmoil in the Toy Box* (1986) (Pennsylvania: Lancaster. Starburst Publishers, P. O. Box 4123, Lancaster, PA).

Bibliography

Pittman, Howard. *Demons: An Eyewitness Account Placebo* and other publications Howard O. Pittman Ministries, P. O. Box 107, Foxworth, Miss. 59483.

Pratney, Winkie. *Devil Take the Youngest* (Louisiana: Shreveport. Huntington House Inc., 1985).

Sandford, John and Paula. Elijah House, P. O. Box 722, Coeur d'Alene, Idaho 83814.

———*Transformation of the Inner Man* (1982)

———*Healing the Wounded Spirit* (1985) (New Jersey: South Plainfield. Bridge Publishing, Inc.).

———*Restoring the Christian Family* (1986) (Oklahoma: Tulsa, Victory House Inc.).

———*The Elijah Task* (1977) (Logos International, Plainfield, N.J.)

Treat, Casey. *Living a Transformed Life* (Oklahoma: Tulsa. Harrison House Inc. Copyright (c) 1987 by Casey Treat Ministries, Seattle, Washington).

Unger, Merrill F. *Demons in the World Today* (Illinois: Wheaton. Tyndale House Publishers, 1971; Twelfth Printing, 1982).

Walters, Travis. *He Who Laughs in the Heavens* (California: San Jose. Fellowship Ministries, P. O. Box 32752, San Jose, CA 95152. Copyright (c) 1978 by Travis Walters).

White, Anne S. Winter Park, Florida 32789

———*Healing Adventure* (1969, Copyright by author). (Plainfield, New Jersey: Logos International). Available from Impact Books, Kirkwood, MO.

Worley, Win. *Demolishing the Hosts of Hell* (1978)

———*Battling the Hosts of Hell* (4th printing, 1980)

———"Annihilating the Hosts of Hell", *The Battle Royal: Book I, Book II* (1981) (Indiana: Highland. Hegewisch Baptist Church).

About the Authors

Earn Jimmy Flowers is a native of Bristol, Florida, where he now lives. He pastors Life More Abundant Fellowship in Bristol, Florida. He was born again in 1960 during his twenty-one years of service in the United States Air Force after a woman knocked on the Flowers' door while they were stationed in California and invited them to church. The baptism in the Holy Spirit took place in Vietnam. Samuel Moses, now pastoring in Bentonville, Louisiana, but then a Southern Baptist lay minister, led him into the baptism on a discarded pew behind the Ben Hoa air base chapel.

After retiring from the service and returning home in 1974, Flowers attended Chipola Junior College and began a nursery and sod business. He was called into the ministry when he was born again, but did not answer the call until 1980 and entered the ministry fulltime in 1987. He was ordained with Liberty Fellowship of Birmingham, Alabama, under the Rev. Ken Sumrall of Pensacola, Florida.

Gloria Flowers, a native of Georgia, grew up in Blountstown. Both she and her husband completed courses with Word of Faith Bible Institute, Dallas, Texas. Earn attended the Rev. Ken Sumrall's Liberty Bible College in Pensacola. In 1980, the Holy Spirit began to operate through her in the revelation gifts, and she became part of the ministry of sanctification.

The Flowers' have seven children, three of whom still live at home.